A STUDIO PRESS BOOK

First published in the UK in 2019 by Studio Press Books,
an imprint of Bonnier Books UK,
The Plaza, 535 King's Road, London, SW10 0SZ
www.studiopressbooks.co.uk
www.bonnierbooks.co.uk

1 3 5 7 9 10 8 6 4 2

ISBN 978-1-78741-595-9

Written by Alex Riviello

Edited by Matt Yeo

Designed by Grant Kempster

Created by Cloud King Creative

Printed in the UK

APEX
— LEGENDS —

HOW TO BECOME
A CHAMPION

THE
UNOFFICIAL
GUIDE

CONTENTS

© 2019 Electronic Arts Inc.

© 2019 Electronic Arts Inc.

© 2019 Electronic Arts Inc.

ITEMS

KING'S CANYON MAP

© 2019 Electronic Arts Inc.

ADVANCED TIPS

LOOT AND COSMETICS

© 2019 Electronic Arts Inc.

SECRETS!

THE FUTURE OF APEX LEGENDS

© 2019 Electronic Arts Inc.

GLOSSARY

OVERVIEW

WHAT IS

Apex Legends is the latest and greatest in the battle royale genre. It's a multiplayer shooter where you compete in squads of three players and try to be the last ones standing. There are 60 players at the start, but only one squad can win!

The game was developed by Respawn Entertainment, which is famous for the Titanfall series. In fact, Apex Legends takes place in the same universe as Titanfall, although there are no giant mechs (just yet). Fans of the series will find lots of Easter eggs relating to it, though.

Apex Legends is currently a squads-only game, meaning you can't play by yourself. No, you have to team up with two other people to take on the world. You can invite one or two friends to your party to play as a squad, or you can just start a game and be matched up with two random players.

The game only comes with one map so far, King's Canyon, but it's varied and offers lots of memorable locations. Every match is different too, because **the Ring** will force you into different areas of the map.

If you've played Fortnite or PUBG you'll know the Ring as the Storm or the Playzone - it's the damaging force field that squeezes players into an ever-smaller circle of the map. It shrinks down on a random area of the map each match, so you never know quite which way it's going to go. This makes sure that no one can just hide out in a corner of the map, as you're forced to move into conflict. If you stray outside the Ring your health will drop, so you'll have to hustle to keep inside it and watch out for enemies!

Wait a second – why are all these strange-looking people fighting?

If you've played Titanfall before then you're a veteran of the Frontier War, the vicious conflict between the Interstellar Manufacturing Corporation (IMC) and the rebels that fought them. It took place over many years and swept up large swathes of the Frontier worlds, leaving death and destruction in its wake.

APEX LEGENDS?

© 2019 Electronic Arts Inc.

But now the War is over, leaving the many worlds of the Frontier at peace and also without any aid. Without work or opportunities to be found, many survivors relocated to the Outlands, a remote group of planets far out at the edge of the Frontier. While there were lots of resources and opportunities here, it was a rough place to live. It was a place for outlaws and explorers – adventurous souls seeking a better life. However, now that there's peace, that's all been focused into the Apex Games, a violent blood sport that sees entrants from all across the Frontier.

The games have become popular across the Frontier and **Legends** have emerged – famous fighters cheered and followed by millions. Now they constantly fight for fame, glory and money... and so will you!

HOW DO YOU

Apex Legends is available for the PlayStation 4, Xbox One and PC and it's completely free to start! If you really enjoy it there are extra characters, skins and other cosmetics available for purchase, but you don't need to pay any actual money to be competitive in the game.

For PS4 you can download the game for free from the PlayStation Store. Thankfully you will NOT need an active PlayStation Plus membership in order to play.

Xbox One users can find it in the Game Store. You'll need an XBox Live Gold subscription to play online.

PLAY APEX LEGENDS?

On PC, Apex Legends is available through EA's Origin service. You must have Origin downloaded on your PC in order to play, but you won't need to have a subscription service like the Xbox One version. Once in Origin, open up the store and locate the Apex Legends page, where you can add the game to your library for free.

Apex Legends doesn't have cross-system play, which means that if you're on a PS4 you can't play with your friends on other systems. However, Respawn is hoping to implement this feature in the future.

GAME SET-UP

After installing the game and any current patches it might need, you simply start it up. Before you start an online match you'll have to finish a quick Tutorial level that shows you the ropes. Pay attention to this section, as it's the only time you'll get to play with different weapons and abilities without it being a life or death situation.

It's a good idea to check out the options menu before you start. There you can find different gameplay options that change everything from the damage indicators to button hints and prompt styles. There's even a Streamer Mode that will make players' names anonymous.

Apex Legends was built to be as accessible to as many players as possible and so offers a broad range of options. There are multiple colour-blind modes, subtitles with adjustable sizes and accessible chat features.

The modifiable nature of the game continues with the Controller section. Of course, on PC the best way to play Apex Legends is simply with a mouse and keyboard. If you want to get serious, upgrade your equipment with gaming mice and keyboards. If for some reason you prefer a gamepad, note that the PC version supports the Xbox One and PS4 controllers.

© 2019 Electronic Arts Inc.

On the settings screen image (left to right, top tabs): GAMEPLAY, CONTROLLER, VIDEO, AUDIO

Setting	Option	Option
Interact Prompt Style	Compact	Default
Button Hints	Off	On
Crosshair Damage Feedback	‹	X w/ Shield Icon ›
Damage Numbers	‹	Stacking ›
Ping Opacity	Default	Faded
Obituaries	Off	On
Incoming Damage Feedback	‹	3D ›
Streamer Mode	‹	Off ›
Usage Sharing	Disabled	Enabled

ACCESSIBILITY

Setting	Option	Option
Color Blind Mode	‹	Off ›
Subtitles	Off	On
Subtitle Size	‹	Normal ›
Enable Accessible Chat Features	‹	Off ›

Color Blind Mode
Modifies most friend-or-foe colors for easier identification.

Protanopia: Compensates for a red-green color deficit.
Deuteranopia: Compensates for a different red-green color deficit.
Tritanopia: Compensates for a blue-yellow color deficit.

- Enemy
- Squad Member 1
- Squad Member 2
- Squad Member 3
- Loot: Common
- Loot: Rare
- Loot: Epic
- Loot: Legendary

Back   Restore Defaults   Modify   Read User Agreement and Privacy & Cookie Policy

© 2019 Electronic Arts Inc.

On consoles you'll deal with your controller of choice. In the menu you'll find options to modify the button and stick layout, adjust the sensitivity and, most importantly, invert your controls. The game even offers custom look controls where you can truly customise your controls to perfection.

In the Video settings you can adjust the brightness and field of view, as well as minimize the screen shake during sprinting, just in case you're one of those people who gets a little queasy playing first-person shooters.

Audio settings let you change the volume for every aspect of the game, from sound effects to lobby music. It even has a feature that converts incoming voice chat into chat text, which is great for the hard of hearing.

Apex Legends really does benefit from a good speaker set-up, so make sure to set it up if you have it. Headsets are a good idea for communicating with your team, although Apex Legends has an incredible **ping** system that allows everyone to communicate and be a team player, whether they use a headset or not.

OVERVIEW: GAME SET-UP

HERE'S WHAT

Apex Legends is faster than most battle royale games. If you've played Titanfall before, you'll know that Respawn Entertainment has perfected first-person controls, allowing you to easily hurdle over obstacles, slide past enemies and just generally feel like a true superhero.

These are intense, fast fights. Since there are only 57 other players scattered around the map, it's possible you may go a while without actually seeing anyone, just to be cut down in seconds when an enemy team first appears. But the more you play the game, the better you'll get and the better prepared you'll be...

Plus, unlike other games where if you die you're dead, in Apex Legends you have a chance to come back. After death your friends can **revive** you, if you're lucky.

Apex Legends rewards players who stick with it. As you complete matches you'll earn experience that increases your Player Level. Not only will this earn you Legend Tokens that can be used to unlock new characters, you'll also win Apex Packs that contain new skins for your characters and weapons, as well as lots of other goodies.

© 2019 Electronic Arts Inc.

TO EXPECT

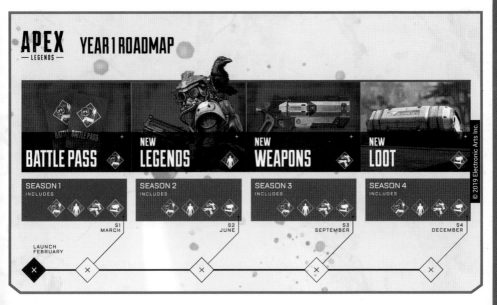

The game is also played in **Seasons**, with a new Season starting around every three months. Each one will offer a new **Battle Pass** that rewards players with new and exclusive gear to show off.

Respawn Entertainment has committed to continuously work on Apex Legends in order to keep it as balanced as possible. Future patches will tweak character and weapon balance to ensure a fair fight as players find new exploits. They also ban cheaters regularly, so don't even think about it!

YOUR FIRST BATTLE

It's time to play Apex Legends! So are you ready for the battle of your life? Of course you're not – but don't stress it! Everyone has to start somewhere...

PICKING A CHARACTER

After pressing the button to Ready Up, you'll automatically be matched with two other players if you don't already have a full squad.

Now it's time to pick your character! In Apex Legends the characters are called Legends. Each player picks their Legend in order, as each Legend can only appear once on a squad. Whoever goes first gets to pick first, but the third and last person to choose receives a bonus, as they get to be **Jumpmaster** and decide where their squad will start on the map.

Since you haven't played it yet, there's no wrong choice of character. All the Legends play roughly the same, all running at similar speeds and able to equip the same weapons and items. The main difference they have is their individual special abilities. If you look at the little icons next to the right of each Legend's name, you can see what their focus is and make a choice from that.

Three bullets indicates an Offensive character – someone who loves to run right into a fight and get their hands dirty. If you like to be the first one breaching a door and never run from a battle, then this is the type of character for you.

A shield indicates a Defensive character. If you like to play things smart and fight on your own terms, pick one of these. You can take advantage of shields and gas traps that can be used to pick off an overly aggressive squad.

A radar symbol indicates a Recon character. So far there is just Bloodhound, a character whose unique abilities allow them to see recent squad movements and hunt enemies down.

A medical cross indicates a Support character. This type of character works best in conjunction with the rest of your squad, helping with healing and movement buffs. Hufflepuffs welcome!

It's the big moment. As with other battle royale games, every single player will start on a dropship that flies into the map from a random direction. A countdown will appear and then it's time to GO!

DROPPING IN!

If you were third to choose your character you might have noticed a little icon next to your name. That means you're the **Jumpmaster**, and you can choose where your team will land. Jump and you will rocket towards the ground, with your two teammates following alongside.

Choosing a good location is tricky. If you leap from the plane early, you're going to find yourself in the midst of a ton of players, which is good for finding better loot, but worse for your survival chances. Finding a further location with some solitude may give you some breathing room, but weaker weapons and items to choose from.

JUMPMASTER

Being Jumpmaster can be a stressful experience for new players, as you will have no idea where a good place is to land. If this is too much pressure for you, you can hold a button to relinquish control, which will assign the role of Jumpmaster to one of your teammates. They'll take the reins and hopefully steer you somewhere good!

On your way down you can break off from your group, which will give you a little boost of speed. This is recommended since you will want to spread out a tiny bit, as you will need all the loot you can get!

GRABBING LOOT

Once you land your first priority is to get a weapon. You are completely unarmed at the start of a match, and while you can melee attack a foe, it doesn't do much damage and is ineffective against an armed attacker. Find a weapon and some ammo for it right away!

Fortunately, weapons are absolutely everywhere. You can find supply bins scattered around that contain two to three items plus ammo, but for the most part you can find 'ground loot' scattered all over the place. One of the most frequent places you'll find it is inside buildings, so open up some doors and head in to any untouched ones you find. There are lots of items and attachments for your weapons as well, but don't worry about what does what just yet.

You'll be able to tell which loot is the best by colour. White items will be Common, blue are Rare, purple are Epic and gold are **Legendary**. Remember to always go for the gold!

LISTENING TO YOUR SURROUNDINGS

Although it's important to scan the world for threats with your eyes, it's just as crucial to keep your ears open as well, as you never know what you'll hear...

One important tactic while you're travelling the world is to simply listen. Gamers who have a Surround Sound set-up or a great pair of headphones will have an advantage here, as they will be able to hear all sorts of things others will miss. Surround Sound can help you pinpoint exactly where an enemy is around you, as you'll be able to hear their footsteps or the sound of them picking up loot. You can also hear when someone performs one of their special attacks and defend yourself accordingly, once you know what to listen out for.

Wherever you are, keep an ear out for Loot Ticks. If you punch or shoot these rare containers you'll usually get at least one Epic or Legendary item. They make a whirring robot sound, so if you hear something strange, hunt around for it and then smash it open for lots of goodies!

Now that you're on the ground and hopefully armed, you've got more dangers to face. Along with the other players trying to kill you, you're going to have to be aware of the Safe Zone.

STAYING IN THE SAFE ZONE

As the Ring comes nearer, you'll want to stay inside the Safe Zone of the map, a section that continuously shrinks down over each round until it's a small circle. This forces all the players to converge on a single point and then makes sure that no one makes it out alive. This is a blood sport, after all!

If you're inside the Safe Zone when you land, you're fine, but you'll have to watch out for players coming your way since everyone will be fighting for common ground. If you're outside of the Safe Zone your mini-map will show you which way you need to go, as well as how far it is. If it's on the other side of the map, you might want to grab your loot and hurry along, as it gets dangerous once the round finishes.

If you do get overtaken by the Ring you won't die instantly, but you will start to take health damage.

Sometimes experienced players will stray outside of the Ring if they spot a place with high-tier loot that's untouched. This is a nice way to be able to grab whatever you need in relative peace, even as your health gets whittled away. You can survive by picking up plenty of health packs, which fully replenish your health, and syringes, which give you 25% of your health back. As long as you have them and keep moving you can stay alive! But it's tricky, so for now you should stay inside and brush up on how the game plays.

You don't need to kill everyone to win a match in Apex Legends, although of course it wouldn't hurt. But for your first few matches you should probably just lie low.

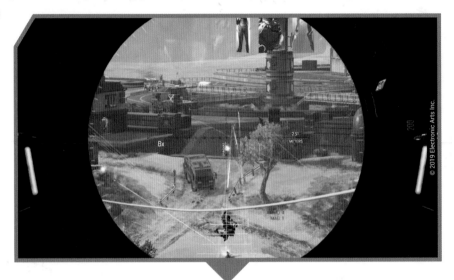

WINNING A MATCH

Don't forget that there are 19 other squads out there, each of which has three members that can knock you down within seconds, if you're unlucky. Even the best squads generally win a match with only a few kills per player.

One thing a lot of new players do is go running off into a battle whenever they hear gunfire. Just because you see enemies across the map doesn't mean you should start shooting at them! Long-range battles are usually a bad idea, unless you're a terrific shot and have a great sniper rifle. That's because it's very easy for enemies to regroup and heal/recharge their shields. Even if you manage to knock down an enemy, their squadmates can pick them up with no problem if you're too far away to finish them off.

As you play you'll have to keep an eye on the time and the number of remaining squads. The game is broken up into eight rounds. Each round has a waiting period in which the Ring does exactly what you think. Then there's a closing period, in which the Ring starts actively moving. Both the game's announcer and the Legends on your team will make comments that let you know when it's almost time for the Ring to start moving, so make sure that you're on your way before it begins. The last thing you want is to be all the way across the map from where you need to be.

The number of squads is easy to see, as it's on the top right of your screen. But note that this number includes your squad, too! So if it says there are two squads left, that's yours and one more. You're almost there!

While it's highly unlikely you'll win your very first match, it's not impossible, especially if you're teamed up with more experienced players. As soon as the last player of the last enemy squad is downed for good it will be official – you're the Champions!

Enjoy the extra experience points and bragging rights and just be warned that the game might decide to make you the Champion squad during the next match. This will make you targets, as players get more points for taking you all down. The Apex Games never end, after all...

BEING A TEAM PLAYER

If you like playing games by yourself, Apex Legends is not the game for you. Respawn has mentioned possibly allowing solo games in the future, but right now you have to play in squads of three. You have to watch out for your team in order to survive.

© 2019 Electronic Arts Inc.

STAYING TOGETHER

The biggest mistake you can make in Apex Legends is trying to do it alone. If you don't stay with your squad you will likely get killed by enemies, most of whom stick together and watch each others' backs. Sometimes you may spread out a bit in order to get the best loot but you should never stray that far, because if you get knocked down a good distance from your friends they won't be able to reach you in time to pick you up. What's more, if you get killed you'll force them to come and try to grab your banner from your kill box in order to **respawn** you. People tend to camp on kill boxes since they know someone will be coming back to help you respawn. Don't make your squad do more work — just stay with them!

The whole reason for having Legends is that each character's abilities can complement the others' abilities. If you're a Support character it's even more imperative that you stick with your squad, but other characters' abilities can work well with different Legends, too. Think about Bangalore shooting a smoke bomb and allowing Bloodhound to use their unique ultimate special ability to see through the smoke and take out your enemies!

Staying near your team allows you to easily share resources. Lots of times you'll end up with items in your inventory that you have no use for, or that your ally might need more. If you head to the Inventory screen, you can drop items that you don't need. Doing that then makes them accessible to others.

The smartest teams share all the best loot they find. Make sure to ping your squadmates whenever you're going to go somewhere so that they can keep an eye on you and vice versa.

THE IMPORTANCE OF PINGING

Apex Legends probably has the best ping system in any game ever made, so make sure you know where the ping button is located (it's usually the shoulder buttons on most controllers). If you aim at the environment and ping it, an icon will pop up on your squadmates' screens telling the other players that you want to go in that direction. What's more, your Legend will speak, saying what they think. If you look at someone's ping you can even ping the ping, which allows you to respond saying that yes, you're going there, or even hold it down to give different answers such as "no" or "I can't".

The ping button is context-sensitive too, which means that if you ping items it will tell your friends exactly what you've found and where to find it. This is crucial, because you want to make sure that your squad is fully kitted up with the best possible gear. If you find an extra weapon or shield and see that one of your teammates doesn't have one, ping it and notify them where it is. They can even ping your ping and call dibs on it so the other player doesn't nab it first!

Holding down the ping button allows you to change what you're saying. You can use it when you see supply boxes have been opened to warn people that enemies have been through there. You can also use it to say that you're going to loot a specific location, or that you want to defend it.

You can even use the ping system to ask your squadmates to look out for things for you. If you head to your inventory and ping an empty equipment or weapon slot, your Legend will speak and let your team know just what you need. Don't have a backpack yet? Ping the spot and let them know that you're looking for one! Need energy ammo? Ping the ammo button on the weapon in your inventory and hopefully your friends will let you know if they spot any.

While it's not nice to constantly spam the ping button (you can thankfully mute someone's pings if they're going overboard with them), if you want to be champions you need to work together and share supplies. Always try to ping smartly!

REVIVING TEAMMATES

If you get knocked down by an enemy, don't despair. You have a little time before you bleed out completely. If one of your squad members can get to you in time, they can pick you up and while you'll only have a little health left, you'll be ready to fight again.

The only problem is that you're a sitting duck while you're knocked down, almost completely defenceless and with no way to fight anyone. That means it's easy for your foes to try and finish you off. If the rest of your squad gets knocked down you are out of the game for good and a "Death Box" containing all of your items will pop up where you were. If an enemy sees you still crawling around they know that your squad hasn't been fully wiped yet, so they'll want to finish you off quickly to prevent a friend from getting you back on your feet, making it harder for them to win.

If you picked up a Knockdown Shield while looting, it can help once you're knocked down. Holding the trigger pulls up a shield that protects your Legend from incoming fire, but it only works as long as you hold it up. It also only blocks fire from directly in front of you, so all that's needed is for your enemy to slide to the side and shoot you there to finish you for good.

Sometimes it's a good idea to hide. You don't crawl fast while you're bleeding out, but if you can find a shadowy corner or drop down into a river, you might want to try and go for it. This will confuse your enemies and allow your allies to pick you up in a safer spot.

On the other hand, if someone on your squad goes down, it's up to you to pick them up. Reviving takes a full seven seconds to perform, so you should make sure there are no enemies nearby before starting to pick them up or you'll have to drop them and try again later. You will only have 90 seconds to revive someone after they've been knocked down, so you'll have to hurry, but make sure that you don't get killed in the process. That won't help your team at all.

If you do die, your body disappears and all your loot ends up in a Death Box, which glows with the colour of the rarest item you had. It might be time to say goodbye to your loot, but you could still have a chance...

If you are killed, you're still not out of the game. Apex Legends allows you to respawn, but it's not easy!

© 2019 Electronic Arts Inc.

RESPAWNING

If your squad members don't revive you in time, they'll still have a chance to respawn you. To respawn someone you need to get to your fallen friend's Death Box and grab their banner from it. You won't have to sift through the contents, thankfully — just go to an ally's Death Box and hit a button. As with reviving, you may want to be sure the area is clear before doing so, as your Legend performs an animation as they pick up the banner that leaves you defenceless for a few seconds.

Now that someone has a banner, either of the two remaining players can respawn you. To do so, they just need to bring the banner to the nearest Respawn Beacon. You may be out of the game right now, but you can hit a button to ping the nearest Beacon, which is a place you can respawn someone.

Respawn Beacons are easy to spot, as they are giant red tripods that have a green hologram of a dropship hovering above them. They are marked with green diamonds on your map and always appear in the same locations every match. Each one can only be used once, so if an enemy uses one, you'll have to find another.

Just like reviving a teammate, respawning takes seven seconds to complete, and you can be interrupted while doing it. As always you'll want to watch out for campers taking advantage of the fact that you're going there to get your squad back to fighting form.

If you're the person being respawned, your troubles aren't over just yet. The dropship comes blazing into the area to bring you back, but it's like you are starting the match all over again. That means you'll have no gear at all. Even worse, enemies will no doubt be alerted to the noise from the dropship (it's not exactly stealthy) and might come running over to pick you off, because they know you won't have much in the way of shields or guns yet.

It's a good idea to have weapons and armour ready for your teammate's return, so they can get ready more quickly. Most Respawn Beacons have supply boxes located right next to them, so try not to grab everything up. Your friend will need it!

You also probably don't want to grab up all of their hard-earned loot just yet, unless it's clear that you won't be able to get back to the Death Box due to the Ring incoming. It's just not polite to steal your friend's stuff.

WORKING TOGETHER IS EVERYTHING.

KNOW YOUR LEGENDS

The Apex Games would be nothing without its Legends. These are the finest fighters the Apex Games have to offer, the MVPs. Each Legend has a distinct personality and playing style and you will need to know about each one's capabilities in order to become a true champion.

GIBRALTAR

Shielded Fortress

Real Name:
Makoa Gibraltar

Age: 30

Passive Ability:
Gun Shield
When you aim down sights, a gun shield pops up that protects his upper body.
Fortified:
Reduces damage taken by 10%.

Tactical Ability:
Dome of Protection
(20s cooldown)
Throws out a dome shield that blocks attacks for 15 seconds.

Ultimate Ability:
Defensive Bombardment
(4m30s charge time)
Throws a marker to call in a concentrated mortar strike.

LEGEND BACKSTORY

Gibraltar started off as a troubled youth. One day he and his boyfriend stole his father's motorcycle and took it on a joyride. This resulted in them crashing and getting trapped by a mudslide.

Fortunately, his parents were two SARAS (Search and Rescue Association of Solace) volunteers and saved him, but his father lost his arm while doing so. This helped Gibraltar know the true meaning of sacrifice. He changed his life around and eventually joined the Apex Games to support his family and became a Legend.

Now he understands the importance of keeping people safe and does so during every Game with the aid of his powerful energy shields.

There are six free Legends available when you get the game and more are unlockable with either in-game currency or real money.

While each Legend plays similarly and can equip the same gear, each one has three unique abilities that change things up. One is a Passive ability that's always on without you having to press anything. There's also a Tactical ability with a short cool down that allows it to be used fairly frequently. Finally there's an Ultimate ability, which takes a while to charge up, but is generally super-useful (and dangerous) when unleashed. Let's take a look at our stars...

LEGEND STRATEGY

Gibraltar is a tank, but that also makes him a huge target – the biggest in the game. He needs to make use of his shield abilities when available, but will definitely soak up some bullets.

His **Gun Shield** has 75 health and protects his upper body from incoming fire. It can be disabled with a button press. You might want to do that while trying to stay hidden, as the glow from it can alert enemies. But Gibraltar should never shoot from the hip, as the shield really helps.

Dome of Protection is a deployable shield that stops all incoming and outgoing damage, yet still allows players to move through it. Note that this does not stop enemies from coming in as well! A great time to use the Dome of Protection is when reviving a teammate, as it can protect both Legends from enemy fire... as long as they're not too close. He can also use it to escape from a tough battle.

Defensive Bombardment throws a smoke grenade that marks an area for a mortar strike. The strikes explode upon hitting the ground and do a ton of damage that can easily take people down if they don't run. This is perfect for flushing enemies out of cover. It can be used defensively, too! If you're surrounded he can throw down his shield and call the strike right on top of himself, which lets him heal while mortars explode around him, keeping foes away.

CAUSTIC

Toxic Trapper

Real Name:
Alexander Nox

Age: 48

Passive Ability:
Nox Vision
Nox Vision allows you to gain threat vision on enemies moving through your gas.
Fortified:
Reduces damage taken by 10%.

Tactical Ability:
Nox Gas Trap
(25s cooldown)
Drops canisters that release deadly Nox gas when shot or triggered by enemies.

Ultimate Ability:
Nox Gas Grenade
(150s charge time)
Blankets a large area in Nox Gas.

Note: Caustic is locked from the base game. He can be unlocked with 12,000 Legend Tokens (which you get from levelling up) or 750 Apex Coins (roughly £5.99).

LEGEND BACKSTORY

You may call Alexander Nox a mad scientist, because that's exactly what he was. He worked at a laboratory and started to experiment with his very own gas on living creatures.

His experiments were eventually discovered by the head of the lab, who confronted him and ended up dying when the lab "mysteriously" went up in flames.

Nox was missing and presumed dead after the incident, but as you'll soon find out, he's finding plenty of new test subjects in the Apex Games...

LEGEND STRATEGY

Nox does his best work indoors in cramped areas. His deadly Nox gas slows and confuses his foes, but since Nox is immune to his own gas he can pick them off easily. His **Nox Vision** allows him to see enemies through his gas, but since your squadmates won't be able to, you'll have to call out their locations.

His **Nox Gas Trap** tactical ability allows him to place up to six canisters that release gas when shot or triggered by enemies. The traps can be placed behind doors to prevent them from being opened. If an enemy breaks the door down, they'll also set off the trap, which will flood the room with cloudy gas. Think deviously with Nox!

In an offensive situation the canisters can be handy as well. If you're cornered by enemies, you should throw them around, as they might get hit by stray bullets and allow a quick escape in the confusion.

The **Nox Gas Grenade Ultimate** blankets a region with a gas cloud when thrown. It's a waste in open areas, so make sure to try to deploy it in cramped quarters. Don't expect to eliminate enemies with this ability as it doesn't do much damage. The gas cloud that emerges from the grenade is about twice as large as a Nox Gas Trap but it still doesn't do much damage. It's best used to keep people away!

35

BANGALORE

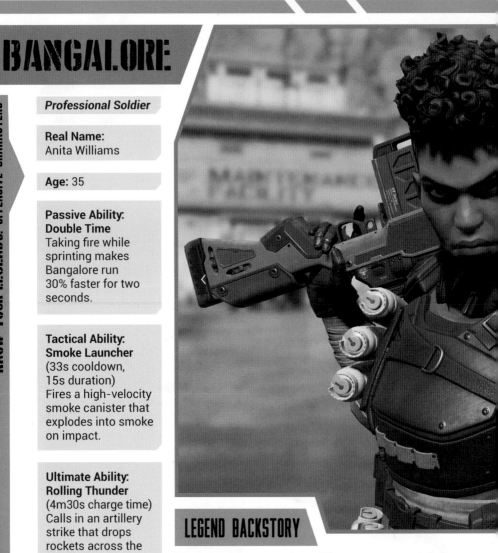

Professional Soldier

Real Name:
Anita Williams

Age: 35

Passive Ability:
Double Time
Taking fire while
sprinting makes
Bangalore run
30% faster for two
seconds.

Tactical Ability:
Smoke Launcher
(33s cooldown,
15s duration)
Fires a high-velocity
smoke canister that
explodes into smoke
on impact.

Ultimate Ability:
Rolling Thunder
(4m30s charge time)
Calls in an artillery
strike that drops
rockets across the
marked area.

LEGEND BACKSTORY

Three years ago, Anita Williams was on a mission to
the Outlands with her brother Jackson, but they lost
contact with headquarters in an ambush.

The rest of the **squad** didn't make it and Jackson
stayed back to let Anita escape. Now she has no way
back home, so she's joined the Apex Games to raise
money for the trip to reunite with her remaining family.

© 2019 Electronic Arts Inc.

LEGEND STRATEGY

Double Time is a passive power that gives Bangalore a speed boost whenever someone shoots at her. Use this boost wisely by running to safety, or to a better firing position.

Her **Smoke Launcher** holds two smoke canisters that deploy smoke on impact. The launcher can carry two charges at a time, and while it can do 10 HP damage to an enemy if it's a direct hit, she will usually use it for cover. It can be used to hide your team and **revive** knocked out squadmates, or to confuse your enemy and flank them. Since this is a launcher from her

shoulder she can deploy it while using a consumable item.

Rolling Thunder throws a flare that targets an area for bombardment. Approximately 20 missiles will thud into the ground before exploding after a few seconds, doing 40 HP damage each. It's great for full-scale assaults, as the sight of the missiles raining down can cause an opposing team to scatter and be easier to pick off. Note that your teammates can get hurt by these too, so be careful where you throw the flare and let them know when you do!

MIRAGE

Holographic Trickster

Real Name:
Elliott Witt

Age: 30

Passive Ability:
Encore!
Automatically drops
a decoy and cloaks
him when he's
knocked down.

Tactical Ability:
Psyche Out
(15s cooldown)
Fools enemies
with a holographic
decoy that lasts 15
seconds.

Ultimate Ability:
Vanishing Act
(2m30s charge time)
Deploys a team of
five decoys that last
for five seconds,
while cloaking him.

Note: Mirage is
locked from the base
game. He can be
unlocked with 12,000
Legend Tokens
(which you get from
levelling up) or 750
Apex Coins (roughly
£5.99).

LEGEND BACKSTORY

A class clown who was a surprisingly good engineer,
Mirage never pictured being a fighter.

He worked as a bartender, living day to day and
perfecting his charming personality. He was content
with this, especially since his two brothers had gone
missing during the Frontier War and he didn't want to
leave his mum childless. But one day she came to him
with customized holo devices and told him to go for
his dream of starring in the Apex Games, which he did.
He's become one of the breakout stars of the Games.

LEGEND STRATEGY

True to his nature, Mirage isn't much of a team player. His abilities mostly help conceal himself or confuse his enemies.

Mirage's passive ability **Encore!** automatically drops a decoy and cloaks him whenever an enemy knocks him down. This gives a few moments to confuse the opponent and hopefully enough time for one of your teammates to pick you back up. It usually doesn't fool anyone, though.

You'll see his tactical ability **Psyche Out** all the time, since it has a low cooldown. It sends a holographic decoy of Mirage that does whatever you were doing when he was activated. To effectively utilise this you need to perform some action that will make it look as if it's a human player. It's also incredible for drawing out sniper fire and determining where an enemy is, or even to scare enemies into thinking someone is coming after them. Experienced players will know what's going on, though.

Vanishing Act deploys a whole team of decoys that confuse enemies, while it cloaks Mirage. This is perfect for situations where you have no escape, or are pinned from multiple sides. While you're in stealth take care not to use your weapons or items, as it will break your cover.

OCTANE

The Adrenaline Junkie

Real Name:
Octavio Silva

Age: 24

Passive Ability:
Swift Mend
Automatically
regenerates health.

Tactical Ability:
Stim (2s cooldown)
Move 30% faster for
six seconds. Costs
10% health to use.

Ultimate Ability:
Launch Pad
(1m30s charge time)
Deploys a jump pad
that catapults Legends
through the air.

Note: Octane is a
Season One Legend
who's locked from the
base game. He can be
unlocked with 12,000
Legend Tokens (which
you get from levelling
up) or 750 Apex Coins
(roughly £5.99).

LEGEND BACKSTORY

Octavio "Octane" Silva was born a rich kid, the son of the
CEOs of Silva Pharmaceuticals. He was given anything
he wanted and became so bored that he took to extreme
sports in order to feel something. He became known for
death-defying stunts and joined the Gauntlet, the course
made famous in Titanfall 2. One day he tried to set a speed
record by propelling himself across the finish line via
grenade. He made it, blowing off his legs in the process.

Doctors said he would never be a competitor again, but he
turned to his old friend Ajay "Lifeline" Che to forge an order
to replace his legs with bionic, repairable ones. Now he's
faster and has joined the Apex Games to get his kicks.

2019 Electronic Arts Inc.

LEGEND STRATEGY

Octane's **Swift Mend** ability regenerates his health non-stop throughout the game, thanks to the dialysis machine attached to his hip that filters his blood. This means you can play more recklessly with him than most other Legends – just dive into a fight and dip around a corner to regenerate your health when needed.

Octane's **Stim** ability allows him to move 30% faster for six seconds, but at a hefty price. It takes a chunk of 10% of his health every time you use it. Since he regenerates automatically, it's usually not that big of a

deal, but you have to be careful when you use it in a firefight.

Launch Pad throws down a bouncy pad in front of Octane that will send anyone who runs over it hurtling up into the air. It can be quite useful for getting your team into a sneaky ambush position on tops of buildings and ledges, but it can also be handy in a defensive move in order to escape from bad situations. Grenades and even other abilities can be bounced off the pads, too.

WRAITH

Interdimensional Skirmisher

Real Name:
Redacted

Age: Redacted

Passive Ability:
Voices from the Void
A voice warns you when danger is near.

Tactical Ability:
Into the Void
(20s cooldown, 3s duration)
Shift into void space, which allows you to move quickly and avoid damage.

Ultimate Ability:
Dimensional Rift
(2m30s charge time, 60s portal lifetime)
Link two locations with portals for 60 seconds, allowing anyone to use them.

LEGEND BACKSTORY

Wraith woke up in an IMC Detention Facility with no memories of her previous life. What's worse, she heard a voice in her head that talked to her all day and night. She fought the voice, but then began to listen to it. The voice helped her realize her power of void manipulation, which allowed her to escape.

Now she's trying to figure out how she gained the power and what experiments were performed on her. There's just one catch – the research facilities she wants to break into are underneath the arenas used for the Games. So she joins the competition in order to find out more about her past, battle by battle.

LEGEND STRATEGY

True to her spooky nature her passive **Voices from the Void** will warn her when danger is near. This is very useful as it basically lets you know when an enemy has its eye on you, even if you don't see it yourself. Since only you can hear it (you're not crazy, right?) you can warn your squad about it as well with a button press.

Into the Void allows her to phase into a parallel dimension for three seconds. You avoid all damage, but you can't shoot. You also can't see other players! It's good when you need to fall back from battle and reposition yourself, or for getting the drop on your enemies.

Her **Dimensional Rift** is useful for both offensive and defensive manoeuvres. When you use the Ultimate it places a portal where you're standing, then you move to place the second one. You'll use up Rift Energy as you do – if it goes to 0% you'll drop it right there. Now both portals are linked and can be used by any player. This can allow you to sneak up on enemies with your full team, or drop back from a firefight when overwhelmed. It can also be used by your opponents, so try not to lead them back!

BLOODHOUND

Technological Tracker

Real Name:
Unknown

Age: Unknown

Passive Ability:
Tracker
See tracks left
behind by their foes.

Tactical Ability:
Eye of the Allfather
(35s cooldown)
Reveals hidden
enemies, traps and
clues in front of them.

Ultimate Ability:
Beast of the Hunt
(3m charge time)
Enhances all senses
for 35 seconds,
allowing them to
move faster and
track enemies.

LEGEND BACKSTORY

No one knows who Bloodhound really is, or even what
gender they might be. There are plenty of rumours,
but no real facts, as Bloodhound has never been seen
without that mask. There are many rumours of what
they really are – a rich person letting their stress out,
a murderer, a former slave, even rumours that they're
actually some sort of half-bat creature.

Bloodhound has the ability to call on Earth's Old Norse
Gods to guide them and seek out hidden opponents,
making them a feared foe.

LEGEND STRATEGY

Bloodhound's passive **Tracker** allows them to see icons representing where enemies went, and how long ago they did so. It can reveal enemy footsteps, doors they've used, players that were killed, or places they've jumped down from. It can be used to help track a group of enemies, if you're in the mood for a hunt.

Eye of the Allfather will briefly reveal hidden enemies and traps in front of them, even through structures. It refreshes fairly quickly and should always be used when you think you hear someone nearby in order to pinpoint their locations.

Beast of the Hunt allows Bloodhound to move faster by 25% and keeps enemies highlighted (even through obstacles) for a while in bright red. This allows them to see through smoke and gas as well! This is perfect if someone is downed and trying to hide – there's no way you're hiding from the Bloodhound.

45

LIFELINE

Combat Medic

Real Name:
Ajay Che

Age: 24

Passive Ability:
Combat Medic
Revive teammates faster and get protection from a shield wall. Also, healing items are used 25% faster.

Tactical Ability:
D.O.C. Heal Drone
(60s cooldown, 20s duration)
Calls in the Drone of Compassion to automatically heal any nearby Legends over time.

Ultimate Ability:
Care Package
(6min charge time)
Calls in a drop pod full of gear that lands in 15 seconds.

LEGEND BACKSTORY

Lifeline was born to war profiteers and ran away from home when she learned of the real-life harm her parents had caused. To pay for her family's crimes she enlisted in the Frontier Corps to help communities in need and has spent her time trying to heal people. But to help people, you need money and that's where the Apex Games come in.

This may seem at odds with her role in these violent games, but with every win she gains funds for the Frontier Corps that helps even more people, and so she sees no issue doing anything she can to win.

LEGEND STRATEGY

Lifeline is the perfect Support character and you should always stick close to your squad when playing as her. She should stay to the rear of the formation. Her **Combat Medic** passive means that she can heal herself quickly and pick up knocked down teammates faster than anyone else, getting them back in the battle when they're most needed. Make sure you're standing in the direction of your enemies, as the automatic shield will only block fire from one direction.

Her BFF **D.O.C. drone** will heal anyone nearby at 5 HP per second, but that means that it will heal enemies as well! So only do it when you've fallen back with your teammates, which will save them having to waste healing items and can get them back up and running much faster.

Her **Care Package** calls in a pod that contains three items, which are generally incredibly useful and occasionally contain **Legendary** weapons and gear. Grab all the Ultimate Accelerants you can in order to speed up the cooldown time. The downside is that it gives away her position to anyone with eyes, as the pod drop is loud and the smoke from it can be seen across the entire map. Try to call it on the edges of the circle if you can, and be prepared to drop back from anyone seeking to prey on your pod!

PATHFINDER

Forward Scout

Real Name:
MRVN (Mobile Robotic Versatile eNtity)

Age: Unknown

Passive Ability:
Insider Knowledge
Access a Survey Beacon to locate the circle location after the currently marked circle.

Tactical Ability:
Grappling Hook
(15s cooldown)
Sends out a grappling hook that pulls Pathfinder wherever it lands.

Ultimate Ability:
Zipline Gun
(1m30s cooldown)
Creates a zipline that anyone can use.

LEGEND BACKSTORY

Decades ago Pathfinder booted up in an abandoned lab and still has no idea who its creator is.

It's been travelling to find more information about itself with no success and finally decided to join the Apex Games. Pathfinder's "thinking" is that if it gets famous enough, it will attract someone who knows what it is. Plus, Pathfinder's really good at the Games.

© 2019 Electronic Arts Inc.

LEGEND STRATEGY

This is one of the trickiest Legends. Pathfinder's all about mobility.

The **Insider Knowledge** ability seems fairly useless at first, as it can only be used at specific Survey Beacons that appear in different locations on the map. Once you find one you can interact with it, which will take around seven seconds. Once finally completed you and your squad will be able to see the next round's Ring location. You won't use it much but it's handy if you want to find out where to head next near the end of the game, when the Ring is getting tighter and you're going to have to dig in for the final fight.

Its **Grappling Hook** is one of the hardest abilities to master, but once you do you'll be able to be one of the fastest people in a match. The grapple doesn't just pull you in a straight line – you can use it to swing around a point and fling yourself up in the air or around corners. You can cover huge distances quickly or simply find a high vantage point with ease once you practise this. Pathfinder can even grapple enemies or other ziplines!

Pathfinder's **Zipline Gun** allows your teammates to get in on the fun. It will shoot out a zipline, and allow you to get to the top of structures or speed friends along when they're running from a closing Ring.

WEAPONS

ASSAULT RIFLES

These are some of the best weapons in the game. They are great against medium to long range foes and are so balanced that you might not need another weapon.

R-301 CARBINE

This rifle was taken from Titanfall 2. It's a handy weapon to start with, but since it does such light damage you might want to swap this out for a better AR later on in the match.

▶ **Bodyshot:**
14 damage
▶ **Headshot:**
28 damage
▶ **Mag Capacity:**
18 rounds

▶ **Ammo Type:**
Light
▶ **Available**
Attachment Slots:
Barrel, Mag, Stock

HAVOK

This AR was released after the game's launch and is the only one to take energy ammo. Since it's an energy weapon it takes time to charge up and start firing, so just take that into consideration before engaging the enemy.

▶ **Bodyshot:**
18 damage
▶ **Headshot:**
36 damage
▶ **Mag Capacity:**
32 rounds

▶ **Ammo Type:**
Energy
▶ **Available**
Attachment Slots:
Barrel, Mag,
Optic, Stock

HEMLOK BURST

True to its name this gun fires bursts of three bullets. You'll have to pull the trigger for each quick volley of three shots. This makes it much more accurate with far less kick, but just remember to keep aiming and squeezing.

▶ **Bodyshot:**
18 damage (54 if all
three rounds hit)
▶ **Headshot:**
24 damage (72 if all
three rounds hit)

▶ **Mag Capacity:**
18 rounds
▶ **Ammo Type:** Heavy
▶ **Available**
Attachment Slots:
Barrel, Mag, Optic, Stock

VK-47 FLATLINE

This is one of the best ARs you can find. It deals high damage and has a hefty magazine, making this one of the mainstays of true legends. You can also switch it from full-auto to single-shot mode, depending on what you're looking for.

▶ **Bodyshot:**
16 damage
▶ **Headshot:**
32 damage
▶ **Mag Capacity:**
20 rounds

▶ **Ammo Type:**
Heavy
▶ **Available**
Attachment Slots:
Mag, Optic, Stock

LIGHT MACHINE GUNS

Want to do the most damage you possibly can? Grab yourself a light machine gun (LMG). They are perfect for medium to long distance battles and can easily knock down your foes, although you'll have to control them. They have crazy kicks and take a while to start firing at full speed.

DEVOTION

The Devotion is an energy weapon that takes a second to start firing, so be careful to keep your sights trained on your enemy as you wait for it to start up. A Hop-Up will help this issue and a stock is crucial to help keep the barrel of the gun from drifting too far upwards while you're firing.

▶ **Bodyshot:**
17 damage
▶ **Headshot:**
34 damage
▶ **Mag Capacity:**
44 rounds

▶ **Ammo Type:**
Energy
▶ **Available Attachment Slots:**
Barrel, Optic, Stock, Hop-Up

© 2019 Electronic Arts Inc.

M600 SPITFIRE

Probably the best LMG in the whole game. The M600 Spitfire doesn't have the slow spin-up of the Devotion and does more damage with heavy rounds. The Spitfire also has superior accuracy, although it still has quite a kick to it.

▶ **Bodyshot:**
18 damage
▶ **Headshot:**
40 damage
▶ **Mag Capacity:**
35 rounds

▶ **Ammo Type:**
Heavy
▶ **Available Attachment Slots:**
Barrel, Mag, Optic, Stock

© 2019 Electronic Arts Inc.

WEAPONS

PISTOLS

While you may be tempted to pass up pistols for some of the bigger, more damaging guns in the game, it might be in your interests to keep one on hand as a backup. They are quick to switch to and can deal the crucial last few shots to take down an enemy during a pitched battle.

P2020

This is the same pistol you might know and love from Titanfall 2. It's a pretty average weapon and not usually one you'll hold onto a whole match, but it can be handy in the opening minutes.

- ▶ **Bodyshot:** 12 damage
- ▶ **Headshot:** 18 damage
- ▶ **Mag Capacity:** 10 rounds
- ▶ **Ammo Type:** Light
- ▶ **Available Attachment Slots:** Mag, Optic

© 2019 Electronic Arts Inc.

RE-45 AUTO

This is a full-auto pistol that will empty its 10 round clip before you know it. Its small size makes for a huge kick, so try to pull it down when you start firing or you'll end up shooting the sky more than your target.

- ▶ **Bodyshot:** 11 damage
- ▶ **Headshot:** 16 damage
- ▶ **Mag Capacity:** 15 rounds
- ▶ **Ammo Type:** Light
- ▶ **Available Attachment Slots:** Barrel, Mag, Optic

© 2019 Electronic Arts Inc.

WINGMAN

The preferred pistol among Apex Legends, this is the only one that takes heavy rounds and it packs quite a punch. It can easily take down an enemy quickly – you just have to be accurate with those shots, as you'll only have four of them.

- ▶ **Bodyshot:** 45 damage
- ▶ **Headshot:** 90 damage
- ▶ **Mag Capacity:** 4 rounds
- ▶ **Ammo Type:** Heavy
- ▶ **Available Attachment Slots:** Barrel, Mag, Optic, Stock

© 2019 Electronic Arts Inc.

SHOTGUNS

Shotguns shoot spreads of bullets, meaning you won't need to exactly hit the player, although it benefits from massive damage when you do. There are no better weapons for a close-range battle.

EVA-8 AUTO

This is an automatic shotgun that shoots incredibly fast, yet doesn't do as much damage as the rest of the shotguns. But it shoots so fast that you don't need great aim, making it good for newcomers!

- ▶ **Bodyshot:** 7 damage
- ▶ **Headshot:** 10 damage
- ▶ **Projectiles per shot:** 9
- ▶ **Mag Capacity:** 8 shells
- ▶ **Ammo Type:** Shells
- ▶ **Available Attachment Slots:** Barrel, Mag, Shotgun

© 2019 Electronic Arts Inc.

MOZAMBIQUE

A laughable weapon. The Mozambique only has three shots, before requiring a reload. Even attachments can't help it much. Give it up as soon as you find something better. Or anything else, really.

- ▶ **Bodyshot:** 15 damage
- ▶ **Headshot:** 22 damage
- ▶ **Projectiles per shot:** 3
- ▶ **Mag Capacity:** 3 shells
- ▶ **Ammo Type:** Shells
- ▶ **Available Attachment Slots:** Barrel, Mag

© 2019 Electronic Arts Inc.

PEACEKEEPER

One of the best weapons in the entire game. Shoots a massive 11 projectiles per shot and is effective far further than you'd expect. Its already-tight spray pattern can be improved with a Precision Choke Hop-Up.

- ▶ **Bodyshot:** 10 damage
- ▶ **Headshot:** 15 damage
- ▶ **Projectiles per shot:** 11
- ▶ **Mag Capacity:** 6 shells
- ▶ **Ammo Type:** Shells
- ▶ **Available Attachment Slots:** Mag, Optic, Hop-Up

© 2019 Electronic Arts Inc.

MASTIFF

This weapon only comes from a **supply drop**. It comes with its own unique shotgun shells, so you'll only get 20 shots with it. It fires eight bullets with each shot, which can each do 36 damage. That makes for 288 total damage.

- ▶ **Bodyshot:** 18 damage
- ▶ **Headshot:** 36 damage
- ▶ **Projectiles per shot:** 8
- ▶ **Mag Capacity:** 20 shells
- ▶ **Ammo Type:** Unique Ammo

© 2019 Electronic Arts Inc.

WEAPONS

SNIPER RIFLES

King's Canyon has so many wide-open areas that you generally don't want to be without a long-range option, which a sniper rifle can provide. If an enemy squad that's better equipped for long-range combat attacks you from a distance, your squad will be at a severe disadvantage.

G7 SCOUT

A common rifle in the game, but a very popular one. The G7 is semi-auto, meaning that it can fire so quickly that it's effective at pretty much any range.

▶ **Bodyshot:**
30 damage
▶ **Headshot:**
60 damage
▶ **Mag Capacity:**
10 rounds

▶ **Ammo Type:**
Light
▶ **Available Attachment Slots:**
Barrel, Mag, Optic, Stock

© 2019 Electronic Arts Inc.

LONGBOW DMR

A powerful rifle perfect for long-range battles, it offers a ton of attachment slots in order to fully kit it out. It has a slower fire rate than the other standard sniper rifles, but you won't need as many shots.

▶ **Bodyshot:**
55 damage
▶ **Headshot:**
110 damage
▶ **Mag Capacity:**
5 rounds

▶ **Ammo Type:**
Heavy
▶ **Available Attachment Slots:**
Barrel, Mag, Optic, Stock, Hop-Up

© 2019 Electronic Arts Inc.

TRIPLE TAKE

The Triple Take fires three bullets in a horizontal row with each shot. This means you don't have to aim as well, but also that it won't do as much damage unless each projectile hits.

▶ **Bodyshot:**
23 damage
(69 if all three hit)
▶ **Headshot:**
46 damage (138 if all three hit)

▶ **Mag Capacity:**
5 rounds
▶ **Ammo Type:** Energy
▶ **Available Attachment Slots:**
Optic, Stock, Hop-Up

© 2019 Electronic Arts Inc.

KRABER .50-CAL.

Only available from supply drops, but when you get your hands on one you'll understand why. It's a bolt action gun that takes ages to reload, but at 250 damage for a headshot you won't ever need more than one.

▶ **Bodyshot:**
125 damage
▶ **Headshot:**
250 damage

▶ **Mag Capacity:**
4 rounds
▶ **Ammo Type:**
Unique

© 2019 Electronic Arts Inc.

SUBMACHINE GUNS

These guns fire at insane speeds, but generally have smaller magazines. They spray quite a bit, so they're lousy for long range engagements, but when you're up close with an enemy they're one of the best things to have on hand.

ALTERNATOR

This may look like a pistol, but take a closer look and you'll realize it has two barrels. This is a full-auto SMG that fires by alternating the barrels, and while it's not the fastest SMG around it will empty the clip fairly quickly.

▶ **Bodyshot:** 13 damage
▶ **Headshot:** 19 damage
▶ **Mag Capacity:** 16 rounds
▶ **Ammo Type:** Light
▶ **Available Attachment Slots:**
Barrel, Mag, Optic, Stock

© 2019 Electronic Arts Inc.

PROWLER BURST PDW

This is a burst SMG that fires five-round blasts. Since there are 20 rounds in a standard magazine, just remember that you have four trigger pulls before you have to reload, and plan accordingly.

▶ **Bodyshot:**
14 damage (70 if all five rounds hit)
▶ **Headshot:**
21 damage (105 if all five rounds hit)

▶ **Mag Capacity:**
20 rounds
▶ **Ammo Type:** Heavy
▶ **Available Attachment Slots:** Mag, Optic, Stock, Hop-Up

© 2019 Electronic Arts Inc.

R-99

One of the best guns in the game. Many people will look at its low damage and ignore it, but its fast rate of fire and large magazine capacity means that it can deal out incredible damage if you land every shot.

▶ **Bodyshot:**
12 damage
▶ **Headshot:**
18 damage
▶ **Mag Capacity:**
18 rounds

▶ **Ammo Type:**
Light
▶ **Available Attachment Slots:**
Barrel, Mag, Optic, Stock

© 2019 Electronic Arts Inc.

ITEMS

ATTACHMENTS

You will need attachments. Pick up a weapon and you'll be able to fight your enemies, sure, but without attachments on it you'll be outgunned in no time. Fortunately Apex Legends makes it super simple to figure out which weapons you're carrying need what

WEAPON STOCKS

Stocks reduce the draw time of your weapons – how long it takes to pull them up after switching to them. They also reduce the amount of drift while aiming, so that your aim will stay on target while you're moving. They come in Common (white), Rare (blue), Epic (purple) and Legendary (gold) varieties. The rarer ones are always better, so don't hesitate to swap the lesser ones out when you find one.

Standard Stock: Weapons: LMG, SMG, AR

Sniper Stock: Weapons: Sniper Rifle

MAGAZINES

Magazines are simple – they just give you more shots before you have to reload. They come in Common (white), Rare (blue), Epic (purple) and Legendary (gold) varieties, with each rarer one allowing a magazine to hold more rounds. At Rare (blue) levels and above, the light and heavy mags also reduce reload time.

Extended Light Mag: All Light Ammo Weapons

Extended Heavy Mag: All Heavy Ammo Weapons

Shotgun Bolt : Shotguns

HOP-UPS

Hop-Ups are rare attachments that only fit to specific weapons and can change their stats pretty significantly.

Precision Choke
Allows you to hold down the fire button to charge up a tighter spread
Weapons: Peacekeeper, Triple Take

Selectfire Receiver: Enables full-auto firing mode
Weapons: Prowler, Havoc Purple

Skullpiercer Rifling : Increases headshot damage
Weapons: Longbow, Wingman

Turbocharger: Reduces spin-up time for energy weapons
Weapons: Devotion, Havoc

attachments and quickly equip them. Attachments can be found scattered all around the world, either on the floor or in supply boxes/drop pods, same as all the other gear. If you aim at an attachment, a pop-up will appear that shows whether you are carrying a weapon it can attach to. Then you simply pick it up and your character will automatically install it on the gun in question. If you swap your weapon for a new one, the pop-up will show which attachments come with it, saving you from having to figure out what each one takes. Attachments can improve every aspect of your guns and come in different tiers, from Common to Legendary, which tells you how good each one is.

OPTICS

Sights are available for any range of engagement. 1x sights are great for close-up battles, while sniper rifles can get all the way up to 10x zooms in order to headshot enemies kilometres away. There are a couple of nifty features optics can come with, too.

VARIABLE SIGHTS

This allows you to switch between two different zooms with the press of a button, all the better to get an overall view of an area before focusing on a specific point.

THREAT HIGHLIGHTING

This highlights enemies in red, allowing you to see them through smoke or gas.

CLOSE RANGE SIGHTS

1x Holo	Common (White)	All Weapons
1x Digital Threat	Legendary (Gold)	Shotgun, SMG, Pistol-Threat Detection
1x-2x Variable Holo	Rare (Blue)	All Weapons, Variable Sight
1x Hcog 'Classic'	Common (White)	All Weapons
2x Hcog 'Bruiser'	Rare (Blue)	All Weapons

MID RANGE SIGHTS

3x Hcog 'Ranger'	Epic (Purple)	AR, LMG, Sniper, SMG
2x-4x Variable Aog	Epic (Purple)	AR, LMG, Sniper, Sniper Variable Sight

LONG RANGE SIGHTS

6x Sniper - Rare - Sniper	Epic (Purple)	Sniper
4x-8x Variable	Epic (Purple)	Sniper, Variable Sight
4x-10x Digital Sniper Threat	Legendary (Gold)	Sniper, Variable Sight Threat Detection

© 2019 Electronic Arts Inc.

ITEMS

CONSUMABLES

Apex Legends has a number of single-use items that you should stock up on. Use them once and they're gone, but they can help you win a battle when used cleverly.

ARC STAR

You can hold two Arc Stars in each inventory slot.

Explosion Damage: 70
Impact Damage: 15
Explosion Timer: 3 seconds

Think of this as a sticky grenade combined with a three-bladed throwing knife. The Arc Star can stick to any surface or player it is thrown at. After three seconds the Arc Star will explode, causing 70 damage to players directly in the blast and stunning them, which causes them to move at a slower speed. If a player is within the blast radius and is shielded, the shields will be disabled.

This means that if you come across enemies with purple armour, the Arc Star can be your best friend. The Arc Star can also be used to destroy doors.

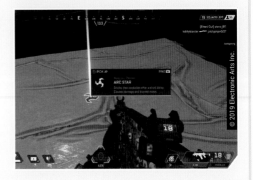

FRAG GRENADE

You can hold two Frag Grenades in each inventory slot.

Explosion Damage: 100
Impact Damage: 10
Explosion Timer: 4 seconds

This is a standard grenade. It explodes four seconds after being thrown and does damage to a player depending on how close they are to the centre of the blast. You can even bounce it off an enemy for 10 damage.

Unlike all the other grenades, Frag Grenades can bounce off walls and roll along on the floor. This makes them great for trick shots, or for throwing grenades around corners.

THERMITE GRENADE

Explosion Damage: 0
Impact Damage: 0
Fire Damage: 4
Explosion Timer: 8 seconds

Thermite grenades are impact grenades that explode on impact into a fiery inferno. Anyone caught inside its horizontal wall of flames will find themselves on fire. While they don't inflict a tremendous amount of damage to anyone who's not knocked down, they are perfect for flushing enemies out of an entrenched position.

They can also be used to dissuade anyone from following your squad while you're retreating. You can hold two Thermite Grenades in each inventory slot.

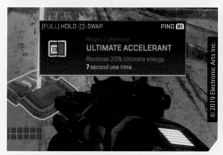

ULTIMATE ACCELERANT

Tip: Give Lifeline this more often than not. Her Ultimate drops a supply pod that can be full of useful items for the team.

When used, this rare item restores 20% of your character's Ultimate metre. It takes seven seconds to deploy, so be sure there are no enemies lurking nearby. You can only hold one Ultimate Accelerant in each inventory slot, so make sure to use it as soon as you can to fill up your inventory with more pressing items.

ITEMS

GEAR

BACKPACK

Level 1 Common (White)	+2 Inventory Slots
Level 2 Rare (Blue)	+4 Inventory Slots
Level 3 Epic (Purple)	+6 Inventory Slots
Level 4 Legendary (Gold)	+6 Inventory Slots Healing items take 50% less time to use

You won't pick up too much stuff before you start to long for a backpack. At the start of a match you can only have eight inventory slots to fill with ammo, consumables and extra attachments. It's not nearly enough though, especially if you're trying to stockpile ammunition or healing items. Backpacks can help. Like all the other gear, backpacks can be found in four different rarities:

BODY SHIELD

Level 1 Common (White)	Absorbs 50 Damage
Level 2 Rare (Blue)	Absorbs 75 Damage
Level 3 Epic (Purple)	Absorbs 100 Damage
Level 4 Legendary (Gold)	Absorbs 100 Damage Performing Finishers fully regenerates shield

Besides a gun, a body shield is the most important item to obtain right away. Shields give you HP up and over your health bar and can be replenished with items just like health can. As with the other items body shields can be found in four different rarities:

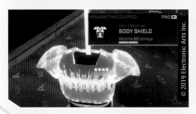

HELMET

Even if you have Body Armour, you can use a little more protection! In Apex Legends headshots do considerably more damage than body or limb shots, so it's important to protect your noggin. You can do that by equipping a helmet. As with the other items, helmets can be found in four different rarities:

Level 1 Common (White)	Reduces headshot bonus damage by 30%
Level 2 Rare (Blue)	Reduces headshot bonus damage by 40%
Level 3 Epic (Purple)	Reduces headshot bonus damage by 50%
Level 4 Legendary (Gold)	Reduces headshot bonus damage by 50% Reduces Tactical and Ultimate recharge time

KNOCKDOWN SHIELD

When your health hits zero and you get knocked down, you're still not out of the game. You are, however, very, very close to it. Your enemies can shoot you while you're down and finish you off and you want to try to avoid that. Besides crawling your way to your teammates for them to revive you, you can protect yourself with a Knockdown Shield. This is a small shield you can raise to fight against incoming damage. It's a purely defensive manoeuvre, but it might give your squadmates time to come and rescue you. As with the other items, knockdown shields come in four different rarities:

Level 1 Common (White)	Provides protection against 100 damage
Level 2 Rare (Blue)	Provides protection against 250 damage
Level 3 Epic (Purple)	Provides protection against 750 damage
Level 4 Legendary (Gold)	Provides protection against 750 damage Can self-resurrect once after being knocked down

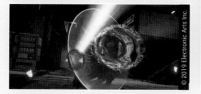

ITEMS

HEALING

In Apex Legends your health works just as you'd expect. You start off with 100 Hit Points (HP) and as you get damaged it goes down and down until you hit 0 HP and are knocked down. Since getting knocked down is one step closer to you losing a match, you'll want to grab cover and heal yourself whenever you can. It's a must after a firefight, but can also be key during one.

To make sure you stay in the battle, healing items are essential. Unless you're Octane (whose health automatically regenerates over time) or have Lifeline on your team (her tactical ability can heal everyone), you have no other way to get your life back. So stock up whenever and wherever you can!

MED KIT

Heals 100 HP   Takes 8 seconds

Med Kits fully replenish your health, but they are rare items. You can see this by the blue glow they give off, plus the simple fact that they're harder to find. You can store two Med Kits in a single item block.

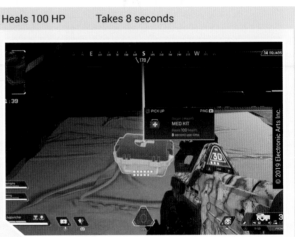

SYRINGE

Heals 25 HP   Takes 5 seconds

Syringes are common items, which means you'll find them everywhere. You can store up to five in a single item stock, so grab all you can. They only heal 25 HP, but they are quicker than med kits, so you can quickly heal yourself during a battle and get back out there. Note that you can cancel healing at any time if danger approaches. Getting shot will force you to stop healing and if the animation hasn't completed you won't get that health.

SHIELDS

Body Shields are crucial to staying in the game, so you'll want to keep them in perfect shape at all times. To do that you'll need Shield Cells and batteries. Each 25 points of a shield is a bar, so you can easily see how many shields you and your squadmates have at any moment and keep them as full as possible.

SHIELD CELL

(Common)   Restores 25 Shield points   Takes 3 seconds

These items work quickly and restore one bar of your shields. You can fit six shield cells in a single inventory slot, so grab a bunch.

SHIELD BATTERY

(Rare)   Restores 100 Shield points   Takes 5 seconds

This one will bring your shields up to full. It takes longer than a shield cell, but might be worthwhile, especially if you have a higher-level shield that would take more than a couple of shield cells to replenish. You can store three shield batteries in each inventory slot.

PHOENIX KIT

Phoenix Kit   Restores 100 HP and   Takes 10 seconds
Epic (Gold)   100 Shield points

These are the beasts. If you are heavily damaged, these are the items you want to use to bring yourself back to 100% fighting shape. The one issue is how long it takes to do it, causing many people to pass them up for quicker items. They also do not stack, taking up a whole inventory slot for each one. Grab a couple to use at the end of a match if you have a big backpack, but otherwise you might be better off to start with Shield Cells and syringes.

KING'S CANYON MAP

Here it is: King's Canyon. This is the first and (so far) only map that Apex Legends has, but it's got everything you could need. There's incredibly varied terrain featuring rivers and cliffs, military bases and airports, underground areas... even a town made of giant monster bones. Getting to know its ins and outs will be key to your survival in the Apex Games.

GETTING AROUND

From the sky the map doesn't appear that big, but looks are deceptive. King's Canyon is a giant place. Picking where to start is key to a successful match, but it's also a bit of a shot in the dark. You never know if a location will have mid or high-tier loot and be worth your time, or if everyone else will decide this is the place they're heading, too.

You also might pick a location that's far from the Ring, causing your team to have to quickly loot on the run in order to stay inside. But thankfully Respawn Entertainment made sure your Legends move fast and can travel easily. You can press a button to slide in order to quickly hurtle down hills and mountains. You can climb to great heights by running and jumping straight into walls, causing your character to perform a wall-jump to the tops of buildings and other terrain. You'll be surprised how easily you can get around when you start to learn the controls!

Even with that, there are a couple of ways to travel around the King's Canyon map even more quickly.

ZIPLINES

Someone has set ziplines up all over the map, which you can grab in order to quickly zoom around. You can shoot while holding onto a zipline, but it's tricky! Some ziplines are vertical, allowing you to head straight up to the top part of a palisade or into a military base, but the majority stretch out across the land in key locations. Don't hesitate to use them to stay in the Ring, although know that you are much more visible to enemy squads while doing so.

© 2019 Electronic Arts Inc.

ARTILLERY

SLUM LAKES

RELAY

THE PIT

CASCADES

WETLANDS

RUNOFF

BUNKER

SWAMPS

AIRBASE

BRIDGES

HYDRO DAM

MARKET

SKULL TOWN

REPULSOR

THUNDERDOME

WATER TREATMENT

JUMP TOWERS

Around the map you'll find these red balloons floating high in the sky. They're connected to vertical ziplines that hang straight down to a metal base on the ground.

If you grab onto the zipline you'll be sent hurtling straight up into the air. Once you get to the very top and hit the balloon it will shoot you out, just the same as if you had dropped into a glide from the dropship. This allows you to quickly zoom around the map faster than any other method! Just be warned that people will be able to see the coloured trails from your jetpacks as you fly through the sky and easily pinpoint where your squad lands.

KING'S CANYON MAP

POINTS OF INTEREST

Before you drop you'll want to see what's going on with the map. Every match a new area is marked out for high-tier loot. That means you'll find better stuff there, but it also means that more people will be there fighting for it. There is also always a supply ship flying around that has high-tier loot both on top of and inside it. Both the ship and the spot that it's going to land are highlighted on the map.

Again, these will be hotly-contested points, full of players trying to get the good gear and hoping for Legendary weapons!

All the other named locations on the map are guaranteed to have at least some loot. Each time you start a new game each location will randomly be assigned loot quality and when you enter a place it will say if it has high-tier or mid-tier loot there. If no one has looted it yet, you're in luck as lots of goodies will be within. If it has been looted, beware! A team may be lurking that is ready to battle with superior gear.

AIRBASE

A popular location on the west edge of the map. It consists of two landing strips separated by water, although there's a handy zipline connecting the two. There are loot boxes on both sides and make sure to check inside the three ships, as they have gear as well. Expect lots of mid to long range engagements here and head south to Runoff if you need more loot.

© 2019 Electronic Arts Inc.

ARTILLERY

This is the northernmost location, a military base that contains multiple concrete buildings. At the southern end there are two massive hangars, as well as two large buildings. A tunnel to the west leads to Cascades, while the southern entrances can bring you deeper into the middle of the map, or a quick exit east towards Relay or the Swamps.

© 2019 Electronic Arts Inc.

BRIDGES

Can you guess what you'll find here? Besides the bridges you'll also find plenty of handy wooden shacks to loot. While there are many ways an enemy squad can sneak up on you here, there's also plenty of cover if they do. Make sure to keep your eyes peeled while entering these kinds of areas.

BUNKER

Some of the fiercest fighting in the entire map will take place here. It has a tendency to house high-tier loot and is a nice shortcut from the west and middle portions of the map, so it's popular. It's a narrow corridor with a few rooms off it, so it's basically a choke point. Be ready with short and medium range weaponry in here. Drops and air strike Ultimates will be worthless, but grenades can help a lot.

CASCADES

This river can be a dangerous place. There are plenty of shacks on the water that can house loot, but anyone on either side of the river will have a height advantage over you. Make sure that you stay aware while looting. A Watchtower that can house high-tier loot looms at the north section.

HYDRO DAM

A big concrete area that doesn't house as much loot as you'd expect given its size. There are a few buildings and supply boxes, but not much else. A large sliding door leads into a bunker with multiple floors that can lead you to the Bridges section.

KING'S CANYON MAP

© 2019 Electronic Arts Inc.

MARKET

An indoor market that can be a great place to find loot. It has multiple destroyed storefronts and one cool Easter egg (check the Secrets section for more on that!). Be prepared for close-range engagements in here and be extremely careful while exiting. There are two openings on the roof that you can drop into or escape via.

© 2019 Electronic Arts Inc.

RELAY

This is far away from the usual action, but given that it can frequently offer high-tier loot it has become a popular Jumpmaster choice. Be very careful around the river, as if you fall in you will instantly die. Make sure you know Octane and Pathfinder's tactical abilities before engaging them here and accidentally falling to your death.

© 2019 Electronic Arts Inc.

REPULSOR

Located in the southeast section of the map, right under the Hydro Dam. It's a military base similar to Artillery, but with the benefit of a tunnel running underneath it that can be used for daring escapes.

RUNOFF

Nothing like a sewage treatment plant to attract lots of... well, Legends. This location is just south of the Slum Lakes in the northwest corner of the map. It's got lots of buildings that are connected by bridges, offering a closer engagement than other places. You generally won't stay long in this place, but not because it stinks — it can be full of high-tier loot as well.

SLUM LAKES

Popular for those who want to take it easy, this is located in the northwest corner of the map and has plenty of buildings to loot, as long as you don't mind wading through the muck. (Remember Runoff? This is where the sewage actually runs off to.) But this can be a quieter area to stock up the entire team, while you let the rest of the headstrong folks whittle their own numbers down.

SKULL TOWN

This is not the place to go if you want a quiet day. In a recent official poll by Respawn, Skull Town rated as the most popular location in the entire game, by a good amount. There's a reason for that — it's a town built among the looming bones of a giant monster and how cool is that? It's chock full of buildings that house enough loot for your entire team and usually is good for a frantic battle first thing in the match.

KING'S CANYON MAP

© 2019 Electronic Arts Inc.

SWAMPS

This area is dreary and yucky and can be full of good loot. It's a bunch of houses on stilts and you might want to stay out of the water in case anyone is hiding out in higher ground. The southern area leads right to Hydro Dam and Repulsor and can be a choke point for anyone trying to move inland.

© 2019 Electronic Arts Inc.

THE PITT

This area is a tiny little circle inside a canyon, only accessible through three narrow paths. If you're claustrophobic, you might want to stay out. There are only a few supply bins inside, but it does tend to house high-tier loot, so people end up trying to go through there just to see if anyone's nabbed eveything already.

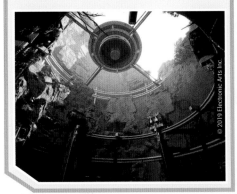

© 2019 Electronic Arts Inc.

THUNDERDOME

This is a high-tier loot area that you won't want to go beyond. It tends to be oddly quiet at the beginning of a match if you want to loot in peace. There are lots of cages holding loot, which is great as long as you don't think too long on their original purposes. There's a lot of vertical terrain here too, such as a spiral staircase going up a tower and a giant hanging cage.

WATER TREATMENT

Another location that can be a little quieter at the beginning of a match, even though it generally has mid to high-tier loot. It's located all the way to the south of the map. There's nothing around the water treatment vats along its north, but there's plenty of loot inside the buildings, as well as tons of supply bins located outside. Its one downside is its distance from your next location.

WETLANDS

Probably the weakest location of King's Canyon, the Wetlands usually has mid-tier loot at most. Its one use can be during a firefight, as it offers a lot of protection from outside attacks. But you likely won't make this a return destination unless you're travelling through it.

ADVANCED TIPS AND TRICKS:
BEST TEAM COMPOSITIONS

While a team of fantastic players will work together no matter what, some Legends' abilities just fit together perfectly. There's nothing like playing with a squad that understands how best to use their unique tactical and ultimate abilities, especially in conjunction with your own. Once you start to realize how they can complement each other, you'll be unstoppable.

BANGALORE/BLOODHOUND/CAUSTIC — SOW CONFUSION

Bangalore's smoke and Caustic's gas can even confuse squadmates, but Bloodhound's Ultimate allows them to see enemies in the haze and take them out. Bloodhound can also ping enemies to let friends engage. The other players need to always listen to audio cues, because if you hear an enemy Bloodhound roar their Ultimate, you do NOT want to release smoke – this will only aid your foe.

© 2019 Electronic Arts Inc.

CAUSTIC/LIFELINE/GIBRALTAR — THE PERFECT DEFENCE

Pick a house to hole up in. Caustic can block the doors with his gas traps, while Lifeline heals and Gibraltar peeks out of windows. If enemy squads get too close, Gibraltar can lay down his Ultimate bombardment and force them to either get hit by the incoming bombs, or push through into the house and into the traps.

© 2019 Electronic Arts Inc.

WRAITH/LIFELINE/CAUSTIC — IN AND OUT

Drop a portal with Wraith and get her close to a battle. Have Caustic drop a trap at the entry point, just in case enemies back through it. Now fight at the other end of the portal. If someone goes down they can teleport back to safety and Lifeline can easily move back and forth to heal anyone who needs it!

© 2019 Electronic Arts Inc.

GIBRALTAR/BANGALORE/LIFELINE — SHOCK AND AWE

Lifeline's **Supply Drop** Ultimate is one of the best in the game, but it attracts enemies like nothing else. Thankfully Gibraltar can cover you with a shield and Bangalore and Gibraltar's Ultimates drop bombs on enemies. You can also use a drop pod as bait and destroy anyone coming to take your stuff.

© 2019 Electronic Arts Inc.

BLOODHOUND/CAUSTIC/ MIRAGE — TRICKS AND TRAPS

Caustic's traps work best when you lure an enemy in and Mirage's decoy can do just that. Once an enemy is lured into a choking fog, Bloodhound can use their Ultimate to see through it and knock them down.

© 2019 Electronic Arts Inc.

PATHFINDER/OCTANE/ MIRAGE — 360° ATTACK

This team excels at movement and at sneaking around to flank enemies or get the literal drop on them. Pathfinder can easily zip around with its grapple, while Octane can launch his team on top of buildings with bounce pads. Mirage can confuse enemies into heading into an area where you have a vertical advantage, allowing you to pepper them with grenades and bullets.

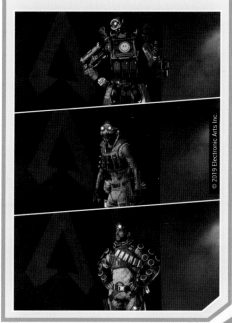

© 2019 Electronic Arts Inc.

ADVANCED TIPS AND TRICKS:
BEST WEAPONS LOADOUTS

You can only carry two weapons at a time in Apex Legends, so choosing a combination that gives you a range of fighting options is a smart idea. After all, if you only have two shotguns, what are you going to do when an enemy squad traps you with sniper fire? Sometimes you'll change your choice of weapon depending on what attachments you find (the right Hop-Up can make a mediocre weapon an incredible one in the right hands), but here are some good combos to look out for.

FLATLINE AND EVA-8 AUTO

This is the combo for first-timers who are still getting used to how the weapons work, since neither weapon relies on accuracy. The Flatline is a very decent assault rifle that does a lot of damage and can fend off attackers at a nice distance. The EVA-8 isn't as powerful or far-reaching as our favourite shotgun (the Peacekeeper), but it makes up for that with a high rate of fire that ensures you'll be able to keep shooting and shooting.

© 2019 Electronic Arts Inc.

© 2019 Electronic Arts Inc.

R-99 AND PEACEKEEPER

The R-99 is a super popular weapon and with good reason. It's versatile and powerful and spits out a lot of bullets. You can use it as a medium range weapon and then finish off anyone dumb enough to get closer with the raw power of the Peacekeeper.

R-99 AND G-7 SCOUT

This combo makes sure you only have to worry about collecting Light Ammo and offers enough options for most fights. Hook up the G-7 Scout with plenty of attachments, such as a sniper scope, and you'll have a weapon to attack from far away and then be able to swap to the R-99 for close to medium range fights.

© 2019 Electronic Arts Inc.

SPITFIRE AND WINGMAN

The Spitfire is the best LMG in the game – an absolutely devastating beast. But its kick means you'll have to fight to control it, even with a stabilizer. For better accuracy a Wingman is a surprisingly good option. This pistol only carries six bullets, unless you upgrade it with an attachment, but each shot does a ton of damage. This is only a good option for people who can aim well, since you can get cut down easily while trying to line up a shot. Both of these use heavy ammo, so you won't have to worry about collecting different types, but the Spitfire absolutely chews up bullets, so grab whatever ammo you can find.

© 2019 Electronic Arts Inc.

WINGMAN AND PEACEKEEPER

These two weapons pack the biggest punch, so they work together nicely. However, you'll need to know what you're doing. They are slow shooting weapons, so you have to make sure every shot counts, but with this option you'll be able to take down enemies faster than they know what's happening. They also don't take much in the way of ammo, so you'll be good with just a few shotgun shells and heavy ammo slots, leaving inventory slots free for grenades and other items.

© 2019 Electronic Arts Inc.

DEVOTION AND PROWLER

This is the Hop-Up dream team-up. That's if you can find a Turbocharger for the Devotion (which makes it start firing without that awful few seconds it usually takes to start shooting) and the Selectfire Receiver for the Prowler, makes it one of the strongest SMGs in the game. Both weapons are not suited for accuracy, but with the amount of powerful rounds you'll be shooting you won't need any. If you can't find these Hop-Ups, you might want to switch to another combo.

© 2019 Electronic Arts Inc.

ADVANCED TIPS AND TRICKS:
HOT ZONES

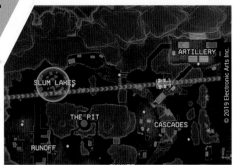

Do you have what it takes to survive a Hot Zone? At the start of every match a random location is marked with a blue circle marker. This means that this is the Hot Zone, where there is guaranteed to be high-tier loot. It's also a place where you can find a Legendary weapon.

The Legendary weapons found in Hot Zones are stock weapons that come equipped with every possible attachment, each of which will be at a Legendary level. This guarantees that you'll never need another gun for the rest of the game – there's no upgrading it. This is a fully-kitted weapon and will earn you the achievement/trophy if you haven't received it already. Keep an eye out for weapons shining gold and nab them before anyone else. While it isn't impossible to find one outside of a Hot Zone, it's improbable. These are very, very rare, and so the Hot Zone will be your best option for getting your hands on one.

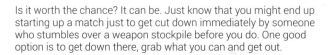

Of course, that's if you survive. The Hot Zone is almost always a spot for intense fighting, usually from the beginning of the match. If you drop into a normal location you won't know the loot tier of the area until you land, but Hot Zones are guaranteed to house the best loot.

Is it worth the chance? It can be. Just know that you might end up starting up a match just to get cut down immediately by someone who stumbles over a weapon stockpile before you do. One good option is to get down there, grab what you can and get out.

If you end up dropping in near a Hot Zone you can stock up on equipment before heading over to see what's left, but you run the chance that a squad or two has already made off with the best stuff.

ADVANCED TIPS AND TRICKS:
SUPPLY SHIP

Lots of new players are drawn to this floating ship and its promise of goodies within. Lots of players have died because of this decision.

© 2019 Electronic Arts Inc.

Imagine the **Supply Ship** as a floating Hot Zone. Inside the ship and on top of it lie guaranteed loot, lots of weapons and gear that can get you ready to fight from the first minute. It's a place that everyone wants to go and is almost guaranteed to be a contested spot from minute one.

© 2019 Electronic Arts Inc.

Not only will the Supply Ship be marked on your map before you drop, but you'll be able to see where it's heading as well. It flies in from a different direction each match and selects a new place to land. Once it gets to its destination it will hover in the air, dropping ziplines down to the ground to aid anyone wishing to see what treats lie within it.

The moment it lands it might be empty, though. Lots of people attempt to dash to the Supply Ship and grab loot before running off, so there might be nothing left by the time it gets to where it's going.

So your best bet is to jump straight to the Supply Ship. But first you'll have to get there. Inexperienced Jumpmasters miss the ship all the time, undershooting it or even smashing their team into the side of it, dropping them to the ground below. Make sure to stay above it and lead it, because it moves faster than you think.

Once you land, make sure your momentum doesn't make you fly right off after landing. While there's no fall damage in Apex Legends, you'll still feel like a fool.

Actually land on the ship? Congrats – and now MOVE. If you don't grab up equipment as fast as you can press the button, someone else will. And then they'll have guns, with which they'll shoot you. If the fight gets too intense, just make a leap of faith and continue your search for loot on the ground.

The Supply Ship is usually chock-full of high-tier gear, and can contain Legendary, fully-kitted weapons just like Hot Zones. The usual trick is to try and grab things off the main deck and then run, although you can find goodies inside the ship too. Being that the area is so popular you might want to make sure your entire team is with you for backup.

If you do end up coming across a Supply Ship later on in your travels, it still might be worth a peek. Once in a while they are left untouched and you never know if you might find some great gear up there. Just be warned that anyone else in the area might have the same idea as you and could be heading up to it to check for themselves.

ADVANCED TIPS AND TRICKS:
EXPERT MOVEMENT

DROPPING LIKE A PRO

If you're Jumpmaster, you want to get your squad to the ground, and fast. One thing you'll notice is that most people don't just drop down in a straight line. One experienced tactic is to perform a **wave drop**, in which you drop directly down towards the ground before pulling up to glide horizontally, then dropping straight down again and gliding again. You can keep this up until you reach your destination, which will get you there far faster than if you went in a straight line.

But the last thing you want to do is come up short of your intended location. If you're going for a far distance, you're better off just pointing your nose and heading there, since those drops will cause you to lose distance.

There's one more good trick to get down to the ground before anyone else, and that involves turning off your rockets. To do that you'll need to trick them into thinking you've landed. Here's how simple it is – if your squad is near tall cliffs, smash into them. This will turn off your rockets and make you fall straight down. Since there's no fall damage you'll be fine and you'll be down there way faster than anyone else. This is a great tactic for locations like Artillery or Hydro Dam.

LEARN HOW TO SLIDE

Now that you're on the ground, you've got to move. Sliding makes your character move faster than sprinting and has the benefit of making you a lot smaller and harder to hit. Any time you see a hill, go for a slide on it. Sliding is the only way you can run faster than the Ring.

LEARN HOW TO CLIMB

Think that structure is too high to climb? Give it a shot anyway. It doesn't go over it in the tutorial, but you can actually climb much higher than you'd expect. If you run straight at a wall and jump at it while pressing forward, your Legend will wall-jump to an even higher height. This enables you to quickly hurtle over structures and walls and get you up to places you never thought attainable. Having a height advantage is always a good idea.

HOLSTER YOUR WEAPON

You can holster your current weapon by holding down the switch weapons button in order to move faster. You should do this whenever you really need to move, or if there are no enemies nearby. You sprint, slide and jump way more quickly when you have your gun stashed.

SLIDE JUMPING

If you can holster your weapon and know how to slide reasonably well, you can perform this move to really zoom around the terrain. All you need to do is put your weapon away, start running at full speed, slide and jump just before your slide starts to slow down. You'll pop up into the area and then start running again, after which you should slide again and start it over again. It takes a little practice, but it's by far the fastest method of travelling the world without ziplines or abilities.

GOTTA GO FAST

Two characters have abilities that affect their movement.

Octane's tactical ability makes him super fast – way faster than anyone else in the game. When combined with his bounce pads he's a speedy force to be reckoned with. Make sure to get some practice bounces in before they're really needed, as it's very easy to go hurtling in a direction you didn't intend. Also be warned that your opponents will be able to use them too.

Pathfinder's Grapple ability doesn't seem to be so effective at first, until you really learn how to thwip around buildings. The grapple doesn't just pull you in a straight line. You can angle it and use that momentum to really send yourself flying. This means that your opponents will never know which way you're coming from, letting you confuse them and fire on them while they're unaware.

Many other battle royale games focus on sorting your inventory, but Apex Legends has decided to simplify the process.

Before you even pick up an item the game will show you if you need it. If you have the same item or a better one it prevents you from picking it up with a press, freeing you from accidentally picking up unwanted junk. You can, however, pick something up by holding down the button. You might want to do that early on if you run across a high-tier attachment for weapons you don't have just yet, but plan on looking for. Sometimes there's nothing worse than coming across a weapon you found a Hop-Up for and left behind a while ago.

Your inventory is initially comprised of only eight slots and once you start collecting ammo and items it fills up fast, so finding a Backpack is crucial if you don't want to have to leave things behind while you're looting. Each higher level Backpack gives you two more slots to use, which doesn't sound like much, but can give you so many more options.

End up with junk by accident? You can always drop items you don't need anymore and fortunately the game even tells you what items are currently useless to you! If you only have energy weapons, for example, and you look into your inventory, you'll notice that the other types of ammo such as light and heavy will have a red 'don't' sign on the top left. This means that you can't use that particular item, so you should drop it by pressing the appropriate button.

You really should drop anything you can't use, because it's just taking up space from better items that could be of use to you in the firefights to come. If you have a high level item, you might want to ping it so that your teammates can potentially use it.

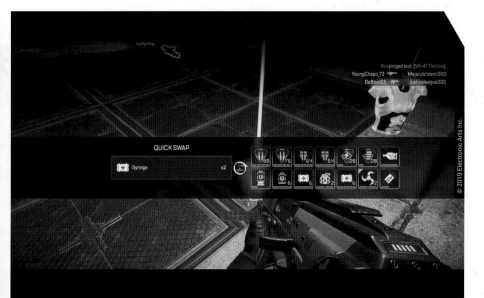

There are a few things that you should always have on hand. You'll want at least two slots full of your main type of ammo so that you never run out and even more if you're using an ammo-hungry weapon like an assault rifle or light machine gun. You'll also want a number of healing and shield items, because you will want to get yourself back to perfect condition as soon as possible after taking some hits. Unless Lifeline is on your team you won't be able to heal any other way. Phoenix Kits are incredible near the end of a match, as they can fully replenish everything you need, but they take up a slot apiece and you might be better off with syringes and Shield Cells in the opening rounds.

If your inventory is full, you'll know it when trying to loot. Little boxes appear on the screen filled in with red to show you how many slots are available without having to go to your inventory screen.

When it's completely full you'll want to finally open it up and see what you can throw out. Remember that you're only as good as the loot you collect, so make sure you have everything you need.

ADVANCED TIPS AND TRICKS:
ACHIEVEMENTS

Every version of Apex Legends has the same achievements, although they're called Trophies on PlayStation 4. By completing certain tasks you'll be rewarded with points, trophies and the respect of other players!

FULLY-KITTED

Description: Equip a fully-kitted weapon.
Worth: 75 points/ Bronze Trophy
How to: This one requires you to be either an amazing looter or very, very lucky. Equip Legendary attachments to every slot on a weapon for it to be fully-kitted and pop this achievement.

KILL LEADER

Description: Become the Kill Leader
Worth: 80 points/ Silver Trophy
How to: There's only one way to do this – get more kills than anyone else in a match. The kill leader can shift over the course of a match, so you have a good chance of getting it if you survive and aim well.

APEX SUPPORT

Description: Win a game as a Support character
Reward: 80 points/ Silver Trophy
How to: You can tell who's a Support Legend by the medical cross by their name. Currently there are two: Pathfinder and Lifeline. Learn how to play as them and win a match for this achievement.

APEX OFFENCE

Description: Win a game as an Offence character
Reward: 80 points/ Silver Trophy
How to: You can tell who's an Offence Legend by the three bullet logo by their name. Currently there are three: Bangalore, Mirage and Wraith. Learn how to play as them and win a match for this achievement.

APEX DEFENCE

Description: Win a game as a Defence character
Reward: 80 points/ Silver Trophy
How to: You can tell who's a Defence Legend by the shield logo by their name. Currently there are two: Caustic and Gibraltar. Learn how to play as them and win a match for this achievement.

APEX RECON

Description: Win a game as a Recon character
Reward: 80 points/ Silver Trophy
How to: You can tell who's a Recon Legend by the radar by their name. Currently the only recon legend is Bloodhound. Learn how to play as them and win a match for this achievement.

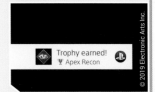

TEAM PLAYER

Description: Respawn a teammate
Reward: 75 points/ Bronze Trophy
How to: You will need to bring a player's squadmate's banner to a Respawn Beacon in order to get this. Make sure that no enemies are nearby to stop you from completing it and getting this achievement.

JUMPMASTER

Description: Be the Jumpmaster five times
Reward: 75 points/ Bronze Trophy
How to: This one is fairly easy. You just have to play enough and not relinquish the Jumpmaster role if it's assigned to you. Drop with courage!

DECKED OUT

Description: Equip a Legendary helmet and body armour at the same time
Worth: 75 points/ Bronze Trophy
How to: You just need two items for this achievement, but they are two very hard ones to find. Hint: Look to supply drops to aid you in this quest.

THE PLAYER

Description: Reach player level 50
Worth: 100 points/ Gold Trophy
How to: Play a lot of Apex Legends. Winning a match gets you a lot of points, but you can also get points by killing other players, or just lasting a long time. After every match you'll earn points towards your next level. Getting to 50 can take you weeks!

WELL-ROUNDED

Description: Deal 5,000 damage with 8 different Legends
Worth: 100 points/ Gold Trophy
How to: Don't stick to one Legend. Play as them all and learn their ins and outs and do as much damage as you can. This means health damage, not shield damage.
Note: This requires you to unlock at least two new Legends to go along with the six free ones you get at the start of the game.

APEX LEGEND

Description: Win a game with 8 different Legends
Worth: 100 points/ Gold Trophy
How to: Simply win a game with eight different Legends —doesn't matter which ones.
Note: This requires you to unlock at least two new Legends to go along with the six free ones you get at the start.

LOOT AND COSMETICS

Customization is what keeps Legends going. It's one thing to win a match, but it's another to have some great loot to show off. There's nothing like being the Champion and having your personalized banner hanging all over the map. Here's how to find the rarest items and make them your own.

COMMON, RARE, EPIC, AND LEGENDARY?

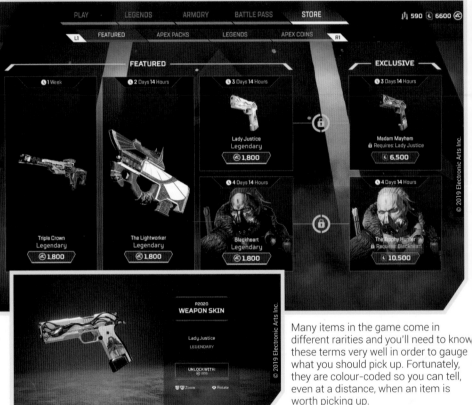

Many items in the game come in different rarities and you'll need to know these terms very well in order to gauge what you should pick up. Fortunately, they are colour-coded so you can tell, even at a distance, when an item is worth picking up.

COMMON
WHITE

RARE
BLUE

EPIC
PURPLE

LEGENDARY
GOLD

Again remember – always go for the gold. Legendary items, whether they be weapons like the Kraber shotgun, or even scopes like the Digital Threat, are almost always worth your time.

Certain Legendary weapons can only be found through supply drops. You will be told by one of your characters when a supply drop is about to occur and you'll see a supply pod hurtle towards the ground. Each drop contains three pieces of loot and it's the only place you'll find the Mastiff shotgun or Kraber .50 CAL sniper rifle, two weapons that come fully-kitted and ready to knock out the most armoured of enemies with just a shot or two.

You'll also want to show off your weapon skins. You can earn these in weapon packs, and whenever you pick up a weapon from the map it will automatically be fitted with your equipped skin. Other players can see what weapons you use and if you drop a weapon anyone who picks it up will see the skin you were using. The reverse always happens and is a nice way of checking out some of the fancier weapon skins without buying them.

LOOT AND COSMETICS

APEX PACKS

Apex Packs are what will keep you playing Apex Legends. While you have access to every weapon and item in the game besides the locked characters, you start off with very plain-looking items. Custom skins offer a chance to make the game truly yours and there are tons of different types to acquire.

Apex Packs look like the Loot Ticks you can find throughout the game and offer you ways to customize your characters and weapons. Apex Packs give you three items per pack, each consisting of these cosmetic items:

WEAPON SKINS
cosmetic skins that modify a weapon's look

LEGEND SKINS
cosmetic outfits that modify a Legend's look

LEGEND FINISHERS
variant animations for executing a knocked down player

BANNER FRAMES
changes the frame of a Legend's banner, sometimes adding animations

BANNER POSES
changes the pose a Legend is performing in their banner

BANNER STAT TRACKERS
A stat tracker used to boast things like your Level, Number of Kills, etc.

INTRO QUIPS
changes the line of dialogue a Legend says during their intro

KILL QUIPS
snippets of dialogue that Legends say whenever they make a kill

CRAFTING METALS
another currency that allows you to buy specific items

Each item is sorted into a different rarity, with the Legendary ones the most desirable. They offer animated banners and skins and are great for showing off your character.
Here's the possibility of getting something greater than Common with a standard Apex Pack:

100%	**Rare Item or Better**
24.8%	**Epic or Better**
7.4%	**Legendary**

You can get Apex Packs one of two ways. You can either level up your character through gameplay, or you can buy them with real money.

As you see you are guaranteed at least one Rare item per pack, but Legendary ones are hard to come by. Thankfully there's a system in place where you can't open more than 30 packs without getting at least one Legendary item so even the unluckiest person in the world is guaranteed at least a few. Apex Packs don't give you duplicates, so you'll always get new stuff.

You will earn by levelling up, although it gets harder the higher your level. You will earn 45 packs up to Level 100, but the rate changes:

LEVEL 1-21	LEVEL 22-51	LEVEL 52-100
One pack every level	One pack every two levels	One pack every five levels

Alternatively, you can just buy them with cold, digital cash. One Apex Pack can be purchased for 100 Apex Coins (about 99p), while 10 Apex Packs cost 1,000 Apex Coins (£7.99).

Whether that's worth the money is something only you can answer – just know that there's no gameplay benefit whatsoever to owning these different skins. It's purely for bragging rights and to feel ownership over your main.

BONUS HEIRLOOM SETS

So you thought that the Legendary items in the game were rare? Think again. Bonus Heirloom sets are the rarest of the rare...

Let's look at the name first. It's called a bonus because it doesn't count as actually opening an Apex Pack. You'll actually receive another pack after receiving this drop.

It's called a set because it actually has three items in one – a themed Banner Pose, Melee Weapon Skin and Intro Quip. For Wraith the Weapon Skin gives Wraith a knife, but it's purely cosmetic. She'll wield it while holstering her weapon and she will lash out with it for her melee attack, but it doesn't do any more damage than just her fists. It does look like it does a lot more damage, though.

How rare are these Heirloom sets? You have less than a 1% chance at getting one when you open an Apex Pack.

Really, really, want this set? Much like you are guaranteed a Legendary for every 30 packs you open, you are guaranteed an Heirloom set for opening 500 packs. Do the maths and that makes for some really, really expensive digital items.

While Wraith is the only character to have a Bonus Heirloom Set so far, more are coming...

LOOT AND COSMETICS

CURRENCY IN APEX LEGENDS

Because games aren't confusing enough, Apex Legends doesn't just have one currency, it has three of them.

First there are **Crafting Metals**. You can get these from Apex Packs, but you won't get very many of them. They're very hard to come by for what they offer and packs usually only give you a handful of them to use.

They are however very handy if you're looking to unlock a specific item.

COMMON	RARE
30 Crafting Metals	**60 Crafting Metals**
EPIC	**LEGENDARY**
400 Crafting Metals	**1200 Crafting Metals**

So they're by no means cheap! But if you want to outfit your character with weapons of a specific skin, this is the way to do it.

Next there are **Legend Tokens**. These are earned every single time you level up. Many levels you won't earn an Apex Pack, but you'll always earn 600 Legend Tokens.

These Tokens are the only way to unlock extra Legends from the game without spending money. Do the maths and you'll realize that to unlock a new Legend you'll just need to level up 20 times to get your next new character.

Unlock New Legend – 12,000 Legend Tokens

Legend Tokens are also used to unlock exclusive cosmetics called Legendary Recolours. These can be found in the in-game Storefront. Generally to buy these you first need to have a Legendary weapon skin or Legend skin and then you'll be able to purchase a new exclusive skin from there. There are two Legendary Recolours available at any specific time, with the selections changing on a weekly basis.

Finally, there are **Apex Coins**. This is where the game gets serious and people drop a lot of real-world money into it. The coins can be used to buy Apex Packs or specific items from the store, but the going rate is crazy for most of the Legendary items from the store (they usually cost 1,800 Apex Coins each, or around £14!)

You get bonus Apex Coins if you buy in bulk, so if you see yourself getting into this aspect of the game it might be a good idea to pick up a more expensive pack.

1,000 Apex Coins	2,000 Apex Coins (+150 bonus)	4,000 Apex Coins (+350 bonus)	6,000 Apex Coins (+750 bonus)	10,000 Apex Coins (+1,500 bonus)
£7.99	£15.99	£31.99	£47.99	£79.99

Again, there is no real reason to spend money if you don't want to. Besides the promise of customizing your character and weapons – and supporting the future of the game, of course – there is no benefit to spending real money on Apex Coins.

SECRETS!

Respawn Entertainment has always loved to include Easter eggs and secrets in its games and there's plenty to find here. While the intense nature of the Apex Games might not give you much time to explore and appreciate these little touches, we'll show you where you can find them.

HOW TO FIND THE TRIBUTE TO SHADIE

This is the game's most touching Easter egg. Lead level designer Jason McCord snuck in a tribute to his dog Shadie, who died during the development of the game. Shadie had been with his family for 10 years and he was devastated. In working through his grief he decided to create an in-game tribute. "Shadie was our best friend and so I wanted her to live on in this little corner of the map," he said on Twitter. "It legit makes me feel better to visit this area sometimes."

You can find the tribute yourself by heading to the market area. This can be a popular zone, so a good idea would be to do it during a match where it's not a hot zone and when you see that no one else is jumping nearby, so you can appreciate it without getting into a fight.

The tribute has a dog plushie sitting on a pillow, with a picture of the real dog in front of it and a picture of McCord and his wife just behind. Players like to pay their respects to Shadie by dropping items from their inventory.

You can also find the dog plushie on the training map, hidden in the mountains. You have to play the training map once before you play online, but you can choose to switch to it at any point by switching to the training map and exploring.

LASTIMOSA ARMORY

We know that Apex Legends is set in the Titanfall universe, but nowhere is this more apparent than in the selection of weapons.

© 2019 Electronic Arts Inc.

The Lastimosa Armory (named after Lead 3D Artist Ryan Lastimosa) is a weapons manufacturer that crafts many of the weapons found in Titanfall. Pick up some of the weapons in Apex Legends and you'll realize that some are carried over.

The Lastimosa Armory manufactures a number of weapons that appear in the game, including the Longbow DMR, RE-45 Automatic Pistol and two Legendary weapons – the Mastiff Shotgun and Kraber Sniper Rifle.

To prove this you just have to look closely at the weapons you pick up, where you'll see the brand stamped on the stock.

A BINARY MESSAGE

If you pick up the PAL 9000 skin for the Peacekeeper shotgun, you might notice a bunch of 1s and 0s stamped on the side of it. Someone with a background in computer science noted that these weren't just a random string of numbers – it was binary code. Breaking it up into eight-bit chunks and converting the ASCII characters to English, it reveals a startling message: "KILL PATHFINDER".

01001011 01001001 01001100 01001100 0001010 — KILL
0101000001000010101010001001000010001100100100101001
11001000100010001010101010010 — PATHFINDER

It makes sense since the skin's name is a clear reference to the HAL-9000, the killer robot in Stanley Kubrick's 2001: A Space Odyssey. That robot acts in its own self-interest after finding out he'll be "killed", so it's clear that whoever wields this Peacekeeper wants to stop Pathfinder from becoming too self-aware. But who made it?

SECRETS!

NESSIE LOCATIONS AND MONSTER ATTACK!

Fans of Respawn know about its affinity for the Loch Ness Monster, Nessie. Every single map in both Titanfall and Titanfall 2 has a hidden Nessie plush figure somewhere in them and Apex Legends continues this monstrous tradition. In fact, there are 10 of them to find! What's more, if you destroy them in a certain order, it will trigger something... massive.

Of course, this is going to be a challenge. The Nessie plushes are hidden all throughout the map and are spread out quite a deal, so just getting to them with the ever-closing Ring is going to be tricky. Plus, enemy squads never seem to understand the importance of your Nessie quest and will constantly get in your way.

The easiest way to achieve this is to do what you should never do in a serious match – split up. It doesn't matter which member of your team gets each Nessie, as long as they are in order. Every time one is destroyed, a note in the kill feed on the top right of the screen will say "A Nessie has spawned", which means that the next one will now be available. The best options are for player one to take numbers 1, 3, and 6; another to take 2, 5, and 9 and the last player to take 4, 7, 8, and 10. This ensures each player will be close enough to the next one.

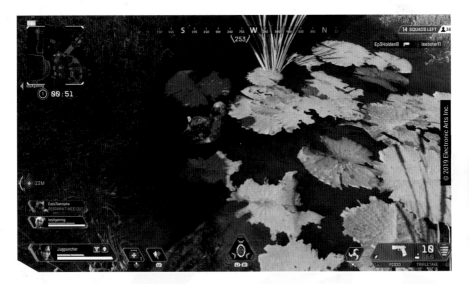

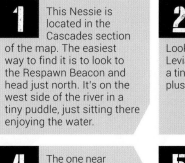

1 This Nessie is located in the Cascades section of the map. The easiest way to find it is to look to the Respawn Beacon and head just north. It's on the west side of the river in a tiny puddle, just sitting there enjoying the water.

2 Next up is a haul all the way south to Skull Town. Look right beneath the giant Leviathan skull and you'll spot a tiny pond with a little Nessie plush.

3 Next you want to head to the Slum Lakes. Look on the western side, where it's floating in the murky water. It's near one of the beams supporting the giant pipes.

4 The one near Relay can be found close to the waterfall on the western side of the location. It's near a Respawn Beacon, in the water next to the cliff.

5 Those disgusting Water Treatment cylinders house the next Nessie. It's in the one second from the east. Unlike the rest it's tricky to see as most of it's covered up, with just its head and neck sticking out of the water.

6 The Respawn Beacon in Runoff is your next destination, located on the east side of the location. This Nessie is once again located in a small pond, this time located right next to a group of supply bins.

7 Now head to the Wetlands. This Nessie is enjoying a bath underneath a waterfall, set in a gap between the cliffs that separate Wetlands from Swamp.

8 East of Hydro Dam is next. There's a Respawn Beacon on the coast. Head there and then go into the flooded building immediately to the west. Look towards the corner inside the building to find Nessie enjoying the destruction.

9 South of Bunker is a group of huts and the next Nessie. To find it look for the most southern hut and explore the rocks just below it, where Nessie will be swimming.

10 Next is all the way to the east side of Swamp. By this point there's a chance that the Ring will have swallowed this area whole, so hopefully you have some health items on hand. It's all the way to the eastern edge near the middle of Swamp. Destroy the plush and look to the water and you'll see an actual Loch Ness Monster surge out of the water. It doesn't do anything else, sadly – it would be a great ally to have in this game! But even at this size – you achieved the impossible! Now get ready to run to the Safe Zone.

THE FUTURE OF APEX LEGENDS

Respawn Entertainment has pledged to continue to support Apex Legends for years to come and considering its incredible popularity (50 million players a month after release!), there's a lot of potential for the game. While we can't be sure of everything that's coming our way, its been careful to lay out some hints of what's in store to get us excited. Ready up, Legends.

BATTLE PASSES

WELCOME TO THE WILD FRONTIER

APEX
—LEGENDS™—

SEASON
01

© 2019 Electronic Arts Inc.

The Apex Games just got wild. Drop into Apex Legends Season 1 – Wild Frontier, then score a season's worth of loot with the Season 1 Battle Pass.

◎ CLOSE

Much like Fortnite, Apex Legends features seasonal 'Battle Passes'. These passes reward regular players by letting them unlock exclusive, limited-time items. If you miss out on unlocking an item while the season is active, you'll never be able to get it again!

The first season of Apex Legends was called Wild Frontier. If you purchased a Premium Battle Pass for Wild Frontier you were given instant access to three new skins – the Lifeline Revolutionary skin, the Wraith Survivor skin and the Mirage Outlaw skin.

That was just the start. There were 110 levels to progress that offered over 100 items to unlock.

Once you unlock an item it's yours to keep forever.

The Battle Pass levels up much like your character's regular level, in which you progress by earning XP at the end of a match. You can earn bonus XP based on survival time, with each Legend having a weekly cap of 25,000 extra points that you can earn. It did this to encourage you to try new characters and not just stick with one.

You can also get an extra 500 Battle Pass XP for your first kill of the day with each character, as well as unlockable boosts for playing with friends.

At level 100 you could unlock a Legendary Havoc Skin called The Silver Storm, which was the first weapon skin that would change depending on how many kills you earned. There was even a bonus at level 110 (for the truly hardcore) that gave you a new badge and a Havoc Rifle Skin called The Golden Idol. It's a good way to show off that you are a devoted Apex Legends fanatic, or that you have a lot of money to spend on a free game.

But you don't need to spend money in order to get in on Battle Pass action. Anyone who plays a season of Apex Legends will earn rewards. For instance, Wild Frontier offered an exclusive Octane skin, 5 Apex Packs and 18 Stat Trackers specific to the season – all for free. You just get many more items with the purchase of a Battle Pass.

SEASON 1 BATTLE PASS
WILD FRONTIER

MAX LEVEL UNLOCKS
3 STAGE EVOLVING LEGENDARY HAVOC SKIN

HOW DOES IT WORK?

- Play matches to level up your Battle Pass.
- The more XP you earn, the faster you level up.
- Earn free rewards as you reach higher levels.
- Earn rewards at every level if you purchase the Premium Pass.
- You can purchase the Battle Pass anytime during the season to unlock all rewards up to your current level.

PREMIUM REWARDS

- Premium Pass instantly unlocks 3 rare character skins.
- Earn exclusive rewards at each level.
- Over 100 rewards, including skins, quips, trackers, Apex Packs, premium currency, and at max level the 3 Stage Evolving Legendary Havoc Skin!

○ Back

The Premium Battle Pass is only available in-game, where it can be purchased for 950 Apex Coins. If time is more of a concern for you than money, you might want to consider buying a Battle Pass Bundle. This gives you a Battle Pack and automatically unlocks 25 levels instantly, but it will cost you a whopping 2,800 Apex Coins. If you ever want to just level up your Battle Pass one level, you can pay 150 Coins to do so.

One cool thing about the Pass is that it doesn't matter what moment you purchase it, you'll automatically earn everything up to your current BP level. So you can sign up at any time during a season and still be able to unlock most of the items.

The Pass actually offers a total of 1,000 Apex Coins for progressing through the entire season up to level 97, which would let you buy the whole of next Season's Battle Pass without spending any more money!

FUTURE SEASONS

One criticism of the first season was that the offerings were pretty slim for the amount of work you needed to put into it. After all, who wants to grind XP just to get a Rare Mozambique skin?

© 2019 Electronic Arts Inc.

Plus, there were no real challenges. The only way to earn new items was to play the game and earn XP and you would earn the most just by staying alive, encouraging people to play it safe.

Respawn has admitted that the first season was made to test the waters and that future seasons might modify the game much further. We know from the roadmap that every upcoming season will have a Battle Pass, a new Legend, new weapons and new loot. But we also think that it's going to add challenges similar to the Battle Passes of Fortnite, that offer different quests each and every season.

NEW
LEGEND

© 2019 Electronic Arts Inc.

Respawn has mentioned that it plan on implementing quests and challenges in future Battle Passes, but for now just wanted to get to learn the game. It's only just come out, after all!

One upcoming feature is a penalty for early leavers. If you leave a game while your squad is still alive you'll start to get a penalty that scales the more you do it. What starts with a five-minute penalty will get exponentially longer. Stay with your team and wait for them to respawn you! Besides, cheats never prosper. Respawn Entertainment has taken great steps to ensure that cheats are permanently banned, going so far as to implement Hardware ID bans that mean that a player can never again play Apex Legends with that computer after being caught cheating. You can expect these measures to continue in the future to clamp down on aimbots and other hacks.

"Season 1 is just the first version on a long road of improvements, updates and tweaks," says Respawn. Expect it to change according to player feedback. They encourage you to contact them and let them know what you think, so work on some (constructive!) criticism and let them know if you want something changed.

FUTURE DLC

So what else is in store for Apex Legends? We have some idea, mostly thanks to a bunch of leaks and data miners who have found information hidden in the game files. Take these with a pinch of salt, but also know it was because of this information that players were able to find out about Octane and his stimpack before he was ever released – so there's potential for all of these!

© 2019 Electronic Arts Inc.

LEGENDS

We know each season will have at least one new Legend. The only one we know anything about is a character named 'Wattson' who is rumoured to be a Defensive class similar to Caustic, as there were strings related to a "Tesla Trap" found in the game's files. Given the name of the ability and the Legend's name, you can bet they will be electricity-based. If they're real!

Here's a list of potential Legend names that have been found. Some of them give you an idea of what kind of character it will be...

NOMAD HUSARIA JERICHO PROPHET
RAMPART CRYPTO SKUNNER ROSIE

WEAPONS

Since many weapons have made their way over from Titanfall 2, there's a lot of speculation that even more are coming. Why not, when they've been tried and tested and already exist in the universe?

EPG-1

EPG stands for Energy Propelled Grenade and it basically launches a grenade of energy that can kill an enemy with a direct hit. It does splash damage as well. This could be way overpowered for the game, but a weaker version could be really interesting.

SOFTBALL

A grenade launcher – another type of weapon that doesn't exist in Apex Legends yet!

DEFENDER

Similar to Titanfall's Charge Rifle, this is a gun that builds up powerful shots.

ARCHER

A lock-on launcher that soldiers used to use against Titans. This is an anti-Titan rocket launcher, so it's anyone's guess how this could work against people.

MAPS

© 2019 Electronic Arts Inc.

TITANS

© 2019 Electronic Arts Inc.

King's Canyon likely won't be the only map. Respawn is undoubtedly working at bringing us new places to battle in and we can't wait to see what sort of varied terrain they come up with. The developers have talked about experimenting with the map's size before release – some bigger, some smaller. They are on record saying that they'll probably release new, bigger maps if they decide they're fun. Let's hope they do.

For a game set in the universe of Titanfall, Apex Legends has conspicuously been missing Titans – the giant combat mechs of that game. But hackers have found unreleased audio files that hint to their inclusion. There are numerous sound files of Pathfinder saying "Titan", as well as the names of different types of Titans, like "Stalker", "Spectre", and "Reaper". Now this doesn't definitely mean that Titans are coming to the game, but it's not outside the realms of possibility.

GLOSSARY

BATTLE PASS Purchasable with Apex Coins, the Battle Pass offers players exclusive seasonal cosmetic items. It expires at the end of a season.

LEGENDARY The rarest items, the rarest loot. Gold weapons and items that you need to pick up.

LEGENDS The characters you play, the heroes of the Apex Games.

RESPAWN Bring a player back to the match after they've been killed.

REVIVE Pick a player up after they've been knocked down.

THE RING The Ring can be your greatest enemy. You'll want to stay within it though, because outside lies only red, fiery death.

SUPPLY SHIP A ship that brings in high-tier equipment. It's high risk, high reward.

SUPPLY DROP Random drops of weapons that come streaking down out of the sky.

MID-TIER ZONE This area will have a decent smattering of items, but you probably won't find everything you need. Still, it will be a good place to stock up.

HIGH-TIER ZONE The best loot. Level three attachments, Legendary weapons – you'll find the best things in one of these areas.

HOT ZONE Guaranteed to be high-tier. Guaranteed to hold an enemy squad or two.

OP "Overpowered". Some people will complain about certain weapons or Legends being OP compared to the rest.

ULT Slang for "Ultimate".

SEASON A period of 90 days that offers new unlockables.

SQUAD Your team, your crew, your best friends.

JUMPMASTER The person who leads the squad into battle. A crucial role that can set you up for success or doom you instantly.

PING Pinging an item reveals what it is to your teammates. Pinging a location recommends a place to go. Ping early, ping often.

SOURCES FOR MORE INFO

Official reddit forum
https://reddit.com/r/apexlegends/

Official site
https://www.ea.com/games/apex-legends/

Official Twitter
https://twitter.com/PlayApex

Official YouTube page
https://www.youtube.com/channel/UC0ZV6M2THA81QT9hrVWJG3A

Official Facebook
http://www.facebook.com/playapex

PS4 Store Page
https://www.playstation.com/en-us/games/apex-legends-ps4/

Xbox One Store Page
https://www.microsoft.com/en-us/p/APEX-Legends/BV9ML45J2Q5V

Origins Store Page
https://www.origin.com/usa/en-us/store/apex/apex

USGamer Guide
https://www.usgamer.net/articles/06-03-2019-apex-legends-guide

RockPaperShotgun Guide
https://www.rockpapershotgun.com/2019/04/08/100-apex-legends-tips-season-1-apex-legends-guide-practical-top-tips-for-all-skill-levels-3/